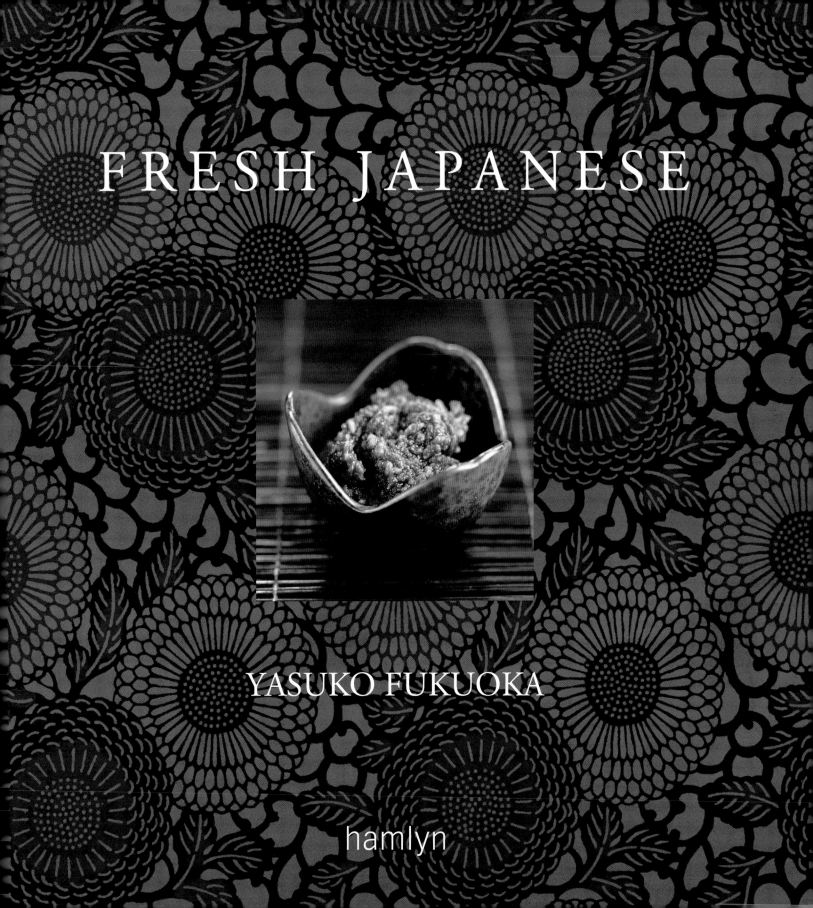

FRESH JAPANESE

YASUKO FUKUOKA

hamlyn

To Paul and Katie-Sai, for sharing my love
of food and life

First published in Great Britain in 2007 by
Hamlyn, a division of Octopus Publishing Group Ltd
2–4 Heron Quays, London E14 4JP

Copyright © Octopus Publishing Group Ltd 2007

ISBN-13: 978-0-600-61641-2
ISBN-10: 0-600-61641-X

A CIP catalogue record for this book is available from the
British Library

Printed and bound in China

10 9 8 7 6 5 4 3 2 1

Note

Both metric and imperial measurements have been given in all recipes.
Use one set of measurements only, and not a mixture of both.

Standard level spoon measurements are used in all recipes.
1 tablespoon = one 15 ml spoon
1 teaspoon = one 5 ml spoon

Ovens should be preheated to the specified temperature – if using a
fan-assisted oven, follow the manufacturer's instructions for adjusting
the time and the temperature.

Fresh herbs should be used unless otherwise stated.

Medium eggs should be used unless otherwise stated.

The Department of Health advises that eggs should not be consumed
raw. This book contains some dishes made with raw or lightly cooked
eggs. It is prudent for vulnerable people such as pregnant and nursing
mothers, invalids, the elderly, babies and young children to avoid
uncooked or lightly cooked dishes made with eggs. Once prepared,
these dishes should be kept refrigerated and used promptly.

This book includes dishes made with nuts and nut derivatives. It is
advisable for those with known allergic reactions to nuts and nut
derivatives and those who may be potentially vulnerable to these
allergies, such as pregnant and nursing mothers, invalids, the elderly,
babies and children, to avoid dishes made with nuts and nut oils. It is
also prudent to check the labels of pre-prepared ingredients for the
possible inclusion of nut derivatives.

This book includes dishes made with raw fish. It is advisable for those
who may be potentially vulnerable, such as pregnant and nursing
mothers, invalids, the elderly, babies and children, to avoid dishes
made with raw fish.

Contents

Introduction
Japanese food has a firmly established reputation as being amongst the healthiest in the world, and the Japanese are known to retain their youthful appearance and to live longer than almost any other people. Although obesity in Japan is now on the increase as the result of a more Westernized diet, including pizzas, burgers and fizzy drinks, people still stay relatively slim throughout their lives.

The Japanese diet is based mainly on the consumption of carbohydrates, fresh fruits and vegetables, and fish; the diet is relatively low in dairy products and meat and really low in fat. Some weight-loss diets take the completely opposite direction to these principles, but this approach to eating became established over a long period and has kept the Japanese healthy. Most Japanese dishes use little or no oil. Deep-fried dishes, such as tempura, were actually adapted from Western recipes and are eaten only occasionally.

Food means health
The Japanese love to eat vegetables and fruits alongside fish and meat. Cleanness of taste is much preferred to fatty or muddy flavours. Moreover, the quest for healthy foods and medicinal ingredients that are not yet known or are long forgotten is actively pursued in Japan because the Japanese believe that eating food is synonymous with taking medicine. Kanten (agar-agar) jelly, black sesame seeds and vinegar are some of the foods that have recently become favourites in Japan, and the reasons they are beneficial to health are often supported by academic research. This concept, *I-shoku dogen* (food as medicine), is similar to the Western idea that 'you are what you eat', but it places greater emphasis on the prevention of illness than on its subsequent treatment.

A feast for the senses and the soul
Despite their concern with healthy eating, the Japanese believe that food must be delicious and attractively presented if it is to be fully enjoyed. 'Food as medicine' should not mean simply a menu based on nutritional values or an extreme weight-loss programme. Instead, it should feature fresh, seasonal ingredients matched by a cooking style that brings out their best qualities.

This book aims to introduce healthy, home-style Japanese dishes to a wider audience. Many of the recipes will not be found on the menus of typical Japanese restaurants outside Japan, and some ingredients new to Japanese cooking, such as sprouted brown rice, are included. These recipes have been adapted to suit the availability of ingredients in the West, and the processes have been simplified where appropriate to overcome unfamiliar cooking styles.

This book is intended to make wholesome Japanese home food more accessible to anyone who wishes to enjoy and benefit from healthy eating.

YASUKO FUKUOKA

How the Japanese eat

Analysers of the Japanese diet usually focus on nutritional values and on the inclusion of unusual ingredients, such as seaweed or stock made of dried mushrooms. This tends to give the impression that preparing Japanese food at home is too difficult for non-Japanese cooks. Is this true? Let's look at how the Japanese actually eat.

The mainstay of the Japanese diet is rice, which is also called *shushoku* (the main meal). Everything else that is served is called *okazu* (side dishes), and at least two different side dishes, eaten in moderate portions, are provided to accompany the rice or its alternatives, such as noodles.

A traditional breakfast consists of freshly cooked rice and hot miso soup, accompanied by side dishes, such as grilled fish or natto (fermented cooked soya beans). 'One-dish meals' – noodles in hot broth, a bowl of rice or sushi rice with various toppings, for example – are popular at lunch.

Dinner usually takes the form of a family or group meal, or the Japanese eat out at a bar or *akachochin*. A typical family meal consists of a soup and three side dishes. Usually one of the three is a protein-rich dish, which Westerners generally take to be the 'main dish'.

At a group meal, family and friends gather together and sit around the table on which there is a large hotpot and a tray with anything from six to twenty ingredients, all to be cooked by the diners as they eat. This DIY-style dining, which includes *temaki* (hand-rolled sushi), is often held at weekends or for celebrations.

In a bar several small dishes are provided to accompany the drinks in a similar style to Spanish tapas.

Finally, at the end of a hotpot dinner or evening in a bar, a rice or noodle dish is served 'to fill up the last space in your stomach'.

Desserts are not usually eaten in Japan. Fresh fruit or a sorbet may be offered, but generally a Japanese meal ends with a small cup of unsweetened green or brown tea. The Japanese do love sweets and cakes, but these usually tend to be eaten to accompany drinks of tea between meals.

Five a day? No, thirty a day!

Another characteristic of the Japanese diet is that small quantities of a lot of different food types are consumed in the course of a day. Japanese children are taught at school that eating 'thirty different kinds of food a day' is the basis of a properly balanced diet, and this wide variety of daily nutritional elements is now widely believed to be the key to a healthy diet.

The 'thirty' include all kinds of fresh foods, from vegetables to fat. They are divided into six groups:
- Protein: fish, meat and soya products
- Calcium: dairy foods, including milk, and small fish, such as whitebait, small sardines and baby eels, which can be eaten whole
- Carotene: green and yellow vegetables
- Vitamins and minerals: other vegetables and fruits
- Carbohydrate: rice, noodles, bread and potatoes
- Fat

About half of what a Japanese person eats each day consists of carbohydrates, whereas fat is generally eaten less than any other food group. Although what constitutes 'one portion' is not defined, as a result of consciously eating small amounts of different kinds of food from all the groups the total food intake per day seems not to reach the level of overeating. The average Japanese man aged between 20 and 50, eats around 2,000 calories a day; women eat two-thirds of that amount.

Even today's children, who eat much more Western-style and processed food than their parents' generation did, have the 'thirty a day' mantra drummed into them, and it comes back when they become adults and start to feed themselves. Most Japanese people try to reach this target, especially those who are cooking at home for growing children.

Eating for health

The fact that Japan has an ageing population makes people consciously seek ways to stay healthy and to avoid being a burden on the health services. This underpins the national interest in healthy eating. The Japanese have a general belief about good food: delicious food cooked by people who care about the welfare of others makes everyone happy and boosts their energy to sustain them through difficult times. If you live to be 80 years old and eat three meals a day you will eat nearly 90,000 meals during your lifetime. You can eat to damage your health or you can eat to make yourself empowered. It is worth broadening your understanding of how to eat healthily and how to create healthy and delicious dishes.

Salt

There is just one problem with the Japanese diet: salt. Both shoyu and miso, the main seasonings, contain high proportions of sodium. Globally, the daily consumption of salt is much greater than it was 100 years ago, and this has serious consequences for everyone's health. Reducing the intake of salt is not as easy as reducing fat in cooking, but there are ways to achieve this without sacrificing flavour, and these methods can be applied to cooking food from any culture.

First, you need to train your taste buds to appreciate the subtle taste of fresh ingredients rather than the taste of seasoning or sauce. Start by eating raw carrot sticks without any dressing or salt. When you no longer crave a salty taste with carrot, start using two-thirds of the amount of salt you usually add to cooking, and then gradually reduce it to a half.

Combining this gradual reduction with changing your ordinary salt to a low-sodium type and ordinary shoyu to a low-salt or reduced-salt brand will help you cut your salt intake by nearly half. Low-salt soy sauces do not taste weak or thin compared with ordinary soy sauce, and they are getting easier to find outside Japan as the leading manufacturers are increasing production to meet the rising demand from around the world.

In the following recipes I have reduced the amount of salt or shoyu from an 'authentic' level. In addition, I use reduced-salt products for salt, shoyu and miso when I cook, and I would recommend all readers to do the same.

Second, learn to taste *umami*. This is the fifth taste after sourness, bitterness, sweetness and saltiness. Long known in the East, *umami* can be described as the 'taste of tastiness'. The main component of this mysterious element is glutamic acid, an amino acid that can be found in a wide range of foods, including seaweeds, vegetables, meat, fish and dairy products.

Try soaking a piece of konbu (kelp) or dried porcini mushroom in hot water for 5 minutes and add a pinch of salt. Compare the taste of the soaking liquid to that of plain hot water with a pinch of salt. Then add the soaking liquid to a soup or to the water in which vegetables are cooked and taste the difference. Once you can identify the subtle richness, your taste buds are ready for their new culinary world. Being able to taste *umami* in fresh ingredients means that you can actually enjoy food without extra seasoning, which will further reduce your salt intake.

Other flavourings Japanese dishes frequently use dashi stock or broth. The stock is made from sun-dried ingredients, such as shiitake mushrooms, seaweed and fish flakes. They are all packed with *umami* to enrich the flavour of the ingredients themselves. Using a good-quality, homemade dashi also helps to keep a dish low in salt.

Umami has always been linked to monosodium glutamate (MSG). When MSG was developed in the 1950s the main aim was to separate the essence of *umami* and re-create it chemically to make an inexpensive and instant flavour enhancer. What the scientists and manufacturers neglected to find out was exactly how a single, free amino acid such as MSG behaves in the human body. The debate about whether MSG is harmful to health or not continues, but many health-conscious people have started to avoid all chemical additives and preservatives. MSG and other additives are used worldwide in processed food, and this is one of the major reasons why home-cooked food is often safest.

A low calorie diet
Many ingredients used in Japanese cooking are diet-friendly, and substituting these ingredients in Western recipes can help you control your overall calorie intake.

Grilled meat or fish accompanied by steamed mushrooms, such as shiitake, shimeji, maitake and enoki, in sake and garlic has one-third the calories of a meat or fish dish accompanied by fried potatoes.

A salad of assorted seaweed with green leaves, with an oil-free dressing, not only fills you up but the high-fibre content also helps your digestive system work better. A handful of soaked seaweed with some chopped spring onions fried in 1 teaspoon sesame oil and shoyu contains only 12 calories.

Jellies made from agar-agar, which is derived from kanten (kelp), stay set at room temperature, unlike those that are made with gelatine. Make 200 ml (7 fl oz) agar-agar jelly with 1 tablespoon of your favourite liquor. When the jelly has set, cut it into small cubes and serve it with yogurt or with fresh fruits. This is a popular low-calorie dessert in Japan.

Mixing boiled and chopped shirataki noodles, which are made of the starch of taro, with cooked rice reduces the quantity of rice but the overall portion volume remains unchanged and satisfying.

To reduce the use of sugar in a recipe without sacrificing too much taste, use half the amount of sugar that is required and add one-third of the given quantity of rice vinegar – for example, if a recipe calls for 3 teaspoons sugar you should use 1½ teaspoons sugar and 1 teaspoon rice vinegar. Mirin, sweet rice wine, has a high sugar content; treat it in the same way.

Presentation
As we have seen, in Japan the appearance of food is as important as its flavour. If you are a newcomer to Japanese food then it is a very good idea to invest in a sharp, good-quality kitchen knife. This makes a huge difference to the preparation and appearance of the food.

Avoid using carved vegetables or fruits, decorative flowers or leaves that are not edible to decorate dishes. Instead, use only ingredients that are part of the recipe itself.

Think about colour combinations. A typical Japanese approach is to combine two or three contrasting colours: red – from prawns, for example – green – from a vegetable such as spinach – and white or yellow – from a garnish such as lemon rind. The recipes in this book mostly follow this style.

Space is important for presentation. Never pile up the food right to the edge of the plate or bowl. There should be at least 2.5 cm (1 inch) clearance around the food.

Equipment
Although most of the recipes in this book can be made in any well-equipped kitchen, if you want to make authentic-looking and -tasting Japanese food you will need to invest in the following:

DONBURI Donburi is the name of a ceramic bowl, 15–18 cm (6–7 inches) across and about 10 cm (4 inches) deep. It is also synonymous with a bowl of rice topped with various ingredients, such as soft omelette and chicken. It has a lid to keep the dish warm.

GRATER The very fine-toothed Japanese grater, *oroshi gane*, is an indispensable tool and is worth obtaining if you love Japanese cooking. Made of glazed ceramic, plastic or metal, the grater is used to produce a juicy pulp from daikon, ginger and garlic. The graters generally used in the West are too coarse to produce the same result.

KNIVES Japanese kitchen knives are mostly sharpened on one side only for a cleaner cut. The most versatile knife is called *santoku* (three virtues), and it can be used for cutting meat, fish and vegetables. For sashimi and sushi toppings, a long, slim knife, *yanagiba*, is used. Its length and shape are perfect for slicing a fish fillet in a single motion.

MAKISU This flexible rolling mat is made from strips of bamboo and is essential for making *nori maki* or rolled sushi. Wash it in hot water and dry it thoroughly after use and before storing.

NABE A clay pot, also called *donabe*, with a lid is used for hotpot dishes. The pots can vary in size from 12 cm (5 inches) across for one person to huge vessels in which sumo wrestlers cook their meals. Most often a pot about 23 cm (9 inches) across will be sufficient for between four and six people. Before using it, fill it with water and leave it for several hours.

OMELETTE PAN A small rectangular pan is used to make the square omelette and omelette roll called *atsuyaki tamago*. Traditionally, the pan is made from copper for good heat conductivity. Before you use the pan for the first time, wash it in hot water, then heat it until it is dry. Pour in some vegetable oil and heat gently for 3 minutes. Wash again in hot water and the pan is ready for use.

PESTLE AND MORTAR The Japanese mortar, *suribachi*, is a deep bowl, scored on the inside to make a good grating surface. They are used to grind nuts or sesame seeds into a fine paste.

RICE COOKER If you enjoy sushi and other Japanese dishes you might want to get a Japanese rice cooker with a built-in timer. Fill it with rice and water and set the timer before you go to work. The rice will be perfectly cooked and ready when you get home.

RICE PADDLE A flat spoon, *shamoji*, made of bamboo, lacquered wood or plastic, is used to scoop rice from a cooking pot or a pan into a bowl or a plate. It is also used for making sushi rice.

Storecupboard ingredients

Many of the ingredients that are used in the recipes in this book are available in large supermarkets, although some of them will be found only in oriental or specialist Japanese stores. If there are no specialist retailers in your area then an alternative option is to purchase the ingredients that you can't buy locally on the internet.

ADUKI BEANS Aduki, or adzuki beans, which are grown in Japan and China, are similar to kidney beans, but in Japanese cooking they are more often used in sweet than savoury dishes. The best way to cook them is to wash 150 g (5 oz) dried aduki beans and put them into a screw-top jar. Pour over freshly boiled water so the beans are completely covered. Close the top tightly and leave the beans overnight. Next day, discard the water and transfer the beans to a heavy-based pan. Cover with cold water and bring to the boil. Reduce the heat and simmer, covered, for 30 minutes. Check the beans by squeezing them between your fingers: if they break easily, they are cooked.

BEAN SPROUTS It is easy to prepare bean sprouts at home. Wash dried mung beans in cold water and put them in a wide-necked glass jar. If you are using soya beans soak them in water overnight. Cover the jar with a cloth and move to a dark place. Change the water 2–4 times every day, and the beans will sprout in 2–5 days. Wait until the roots are 5–8 cm (2–3 inches) long. For a more delicate flavour remove the tips of the roots before cooking.

BENI SHOGA Beni shoga (pickled red ginger) can be used as a garnish for Chirashi-zushi. You can make your own *(see page 21)*, but ready-prepared beni shoga is available from supermarkets and oriental shops.

DAIKON This long, thick, white radish, known as mooli (mouli) in Indian cooking, is one of the most widely used vegetables in Japanese cuisine. Grated raw daikon is used in the dipping sauce that accompanies fried food, grilled meat and oily fish. The juice contains enzymes that help digest protein. Daikons are increasingly available in supermarkets and greengrocers as well as in oriental shops.

Sweet pickled daikon, *takuan*, is named after a Buddhist monk who is said to have invented the recipe. Whenever possible you should choose takuan that has a dull yellow colour. It has a pungent taste and is often used in sushi rolls or to accompany freshly cooked rice.

DASHI STOCK Made from kezuri bushi (dried bonito) or dried kelp or a mixture of the two, dashi stock is an essential ingredient in Japanese dishes. Although it is best made fresh *(see page 19)*, leftover stock can be frozen in an ice-cube tray. Freeze-dried granules are also available. They are usually sold in 5 g (¼ oz) packs to make about 750 ml (1¼ pints) stock. Additive-free brands can be found in health-food shops.

EDAMAME Boiled fresh soya beans are often eaten as a snack to accompany alcoholic drinks.

FISH ROE Widely eaten in northern Europe as well as in Japan, *ikura* (salmon roe) is normally sold ready salted in jars. A popular topping for sushi, especially in the USA, *tobiko* (flying fish roe) is naturally orange in colour, but red, black and green as well as flavoured types are also available. Like ikura, tobiko is sold ready salted in jars in large supermarkets and fishmongers and some delicatessens.

HAKUSAI Chinese cabbage has thick, white, soft leaves, which are tightly wrapped around each other to form a dense, elongated head. The leaves are often cooked in Japan and Korea but can also be eaten raw in salads. They are also used to make pickles. Chinese cabbage is widely available in supermarkets as well as in specialist stores.

KEZURI BUSHI Shavings of dried bonito, a type of tuna, are used in dashi stock *(see page 19)*, but the flakes can also be sprinkled over tofu or boiled spinach to add flavour. Also known as katsuo bushi, it is often sold in 5 g (¼ oz) packs.

KINOME The young leaves from the Japanese prickly ash, from which sansho (Japanese pepper) is derived, have a peppery, anise-like flavour. They are used to add an accent to miso- or vinegar-based sauces and dressings that are made to accompany fish or vegetable dishes.

MIRIN This is one of the essential ingredients of Japanese cooking. It is a clear, slightly sticky, sweet rice wine, made from a mixture of rice yeast, glutinous rice and rice spirit, and it is used to add sweetness and gloss to dishes.

MISO Cooked soya beans are mixed with rice or wheat yeast and left to ferment and mature for between one year and three years. There are huge variations in the colour and saltiness of different types of miso. The basic pastes are brown, which is made from soya beans only and is quite salty; red, which is mixed with barley; and white, which is mixed with rice and is less salty than the other types.

MUSHROOMS Several types of mushroom are used in Japanese cooking, although, interestingly, they are never eaten raw in Japan. *Enoki* mushrooms form clusters of small white caps with long stems at the base of enoki (Chinese hackberry) trees. They have a subtle but rich taste and are delicious when grilled or steamed. Only the cultivated variety – sometimes called sheep's head mushrooms – is available in the West. They grow around the base of oak trees, and the frilly flesh has a smooth texture. They are used in soups and stir-fries and in tempura dishes, when they are deep-fried. Fragrant *shiitake* mushrooms have been widely used in savoury dishes in the Far East and Southeast Asia for centuries. The woody aroma and nutritional content of dried shiitake mushrooms are superior to those of the fresh form. Grey *shimeji* mushrooms grow at the base of beech trees. They are sold still in the clusters in which they grow, connected at the base, and should be separated before being used in stir-fries, soups and steamed dishes.

NOODLES After rice, noodles are the most widely eaten accompaniment and may be eaten with a wide range of dishes. *Shirataki*, which are gelatinous, translucent, jelly-like noodles, are made from yam potato flour. They are often used in hotpots and simmered dishes. Brown *soba* (buckwheat) noodles are considered to be both healthy and nutritious. They are usually available dried but may occasionally be found fresh, and they may be served hot or chilled. Most often eaten chilled in summer, *somen* or soumen noodles are fine and are made from white wheat. Thick, wide *udon* noodles are made from wheat and are widely available, both fresh and dried.

NUKA Mostly used for making pickles, a handful of nuka (dry rice bran) can be added to boiling bamboo shoots to remove their bitter taste.

OSU Japanese osu or su (rice vinegar) is milder than malt vinegar. White, brown and ancient red rice can be used to make different types. *Kurosu* (black rice vinegar) is made from brown rice and looks and tastes similar to Italian balsamic vinegar.

In Japan 1 part rice vinegar diluted with 5 parts water and mixed with a sweetener, such as honey, is a popular drink among health-conscious people.

RENKON Cooked renkon (lotus root), which has a distinctive crunchy texture, is used in simmered and deep-fried dishes and in pickles. It is often sold ready cooked in vacuum packs.

RICE Always use short grain rice in Japanese dishes. It sticks together better than medium and long grain rices, which contain less starch. Japanese rice is sometimes also called sushi rice. You can use dessert rice (the type used for rice puddings) as an alternative.

For *multi-grain rice* mix 150 g (5 oz) Japanese brown rice or short grain brown rice with 50 g (2 oz) of any of pinhead oats, amaranthus seeds (amaranth), quinoa, rye, oshimugi (Japanese pressed barley), hatomugi wheat, millet. Avoid kamut (whole barley), which takes longer to cook than any other grain. Cook as for brown rice *(see page 17)* with the same amount of water. Roasted sesame or nuts can be mixed in after the rice is cooked.

Mochigome (extra glutinous rice) does not contain dietary gluten and is safe for people excluding gluten from their diets. It is very sticky when cooked and can be used to make pound rice cake, mochi and other rice dishes. It is available in health-food shops as well as oriental stores.

SAKE This alcoholic drink, which is made from rice, is used extensively in Japanese cooking and is available in different degrees of alcohol content. Dry sherry can be used as an alternative. *Sake kasu* (sake lees), the white curds remaining after sake is refined, are used to make a sweet drink, *amazake*, or to make pickles.

SANSHO Sansho (Japanese pepper) is unrelated to the black and white peppers familiar to all cooks. Sansho is the ground husk of the pod of the prickly ash (*Xanthozylum piperitum*) and belongs to the same family

as Sichuan pepper. It is not as spicy in flavour as other peppers but makes the tongue slightly numb. It has a superb aroma and is often used in fish and chicken dishes.

SATOIMO This golf-ball-sized potato, a type of taro, produces a sticky slime when it is peeled or boiled.

SEAWEED Many types of seaweed are edible, and each has its own distinctive taste. A type of kelp, *konbu* is sold dried and is most often used in dashi stock *(see page 19)*. Wipe the surface with damp kitchen paper before use but do not allow it to become too wet or it will go soft. Frequently used to wrap around sushi, *nori* takes the form of sheets of dried seaweed. Once the packet is opened, the sheets must be kept in an airtight container or bag or they will get damp and quickly lose their flavour. The soft seaweed *wakame* is generally sold dried. Soak it in water for a few minutes and it will expand five-fold. It has a delicate flavour and is often used in miso soup and in salads.

SESAME SEEDS Both black and white sesame seeds are used in Japanese cooking. The seeds are smaller, plumper and oilier than their European counterparts, and white sesame seeds contains more oil than the black seeds, which have a stronger flavour. The seeds can be roasted, then sprinkled directly on to rice. The husks must be broken in order for the eater to benefit from the nutritional content, otherwise the seeds will be passed through the body undigested. Both white and black sesame seeds are used to make *suri goma* (ground roasted sesame seeds), and which type you use will depend on the recipe *(see page 20)*.

Neri kuro goma (black sesame tahini) is an oily paste made from black sesame seeds. It can be found in health-food shops or food shops that specialize in oriental foods and is more easily obtained in Japan and in the United States than in Britain. If you cannot find it, grind 6 tablespoons black sesame seeds in a pestle and mortar for 20 minutes.

SHICHIMI TOGARASHI Widely used in soups and grilled dishes, shichimi togarashi (seven-spice mix) is usually made of a mixture of dried chillies, green nori flakes, sesame seeds, sansho (Japanese pepper), poppy seeds, dried ginger and dried orange peel.

SHISHITOU This small Japanese green chilli is neither hot nor bitter.

SHISO Also known as perilla, beefsteak plant and Japanese mint, shiso is an annual herb with aromatic leaves, which may be green or red. Green shisho is often used as a garnish for salads, sashimi and tofu dishes; Thai or Italian basil can be used instead. Red shiso has an anise flavour and is used to give pickles a deep pink colour.

SHOYU In Japanese cooking always use a Japanese brand of shoyu (soy sauce) because soy sauces from other countries taste quite different. Low-salt and reduced-salt versions are available and can be used for everyday dishes to reduce your salt intake.

TAKENOKO Fresh takenoko (bamboo shoots) are available for a short time in spring. Once they have been harvested they quickly turn bitter, so they are normally sold boiled and in vacuum packs. If you ever have a chance to obtain a fresh bamboo shoot, boil it whole in plenty of water with a handful of nuka (rice bran). Cook it until you can easily insert a skewer into it, then allow it to cool. Remove the layered skins to get to the heart of the shoot. The soft inner skins may also be eaten.

TOFU This versatile ingredient, also known as bean curd, is made from the 'milk' of soya beans. There are two types of fresh tofu: soft and smooth silken tofu, which is eaten raw or with soup, and firm or cotton tofu, which is used in stir-fries or mashed to make savoury cakes. Drain the liquid from the packet before use. Some recipes require dehydrating by wrapping in cloths and pressing under a weight, such as a chopping board, before use.

Deep-fried thin tofu, *abura age,* can be used as an alternative to meat. Parboil or wash them with hot water to wash away any excess oil and add them to simmered dishes.

UMEBOSHI Salted plums are pickled with vinegar and rice spirit for up to several months, and they are often mixed with red shiso leaves for colour and flavour. Pickled plums are usually eaten on their own or with cooked rice. The ume plum, which is more closely related to the apricot than to the European plum, has rather hard flesh. Umeboshi is

regarded as a superfood in Japan, where it is used medicinally. It helps to lower cholesterol and cleans out chemical additives from the liver. Both umeboshi and umeboshi purée can be found in supermarkets, health-food shops and Japanese or oriental shops.

UMESHU This sweet liqueur infused with Japanese plum is often served cold as an aperitif.

WASABI Although it is not related to European horseradish, wasabi is often described as Japanese green horseradish. The grated root is mixed with shoyu for sashimi or sushi dips and is added to the dipping sauce for soba (buckwheat) noodles. Wasabi has a similar flavour to horseradish but is hotter. Fresh wasabi is rare and difficult to obtain, even in Japan, but powdered wasabi or paste in a tube, which is a mixture of wasabi and horseradish, is widely available.

YUZU This type of Japanese citrus fruit has a bright yellow skin and a strong scent of lemons and quinces. The rind is used to garnish clear soups, pickles, simmered dishes and desserts.

ZA CAI Za cai or Za Sai (Sichuan pickled vegetables), known as *zachai* in China, are the swollen roots of a mustard-like vegetable, which are salted and fermented in an earthenware pot for several years. Rinse off the salt before use. They have a distinctive, piquant flavour and are used to accompany spicy foods.

Menu plans

DINNER FOR 2

Marinated tuna sashimi

Simmered beef with vegetables

Egg soup

Freshly cooked rice
  (white, brown or multi-grain)

Seasonal fresh fruits

LOW-CALORIE LUNCH FOR 2

Clear soup with prawns

Vegetables and mushrooms wrapped in pork

Hakusai, cottage cheese and goji berry salad

Freshly cooked rice

Plum wine jelly with ginger and lemon sorbet

LOW-CALORIE LUNCH FOR 4

Swordfish teriyaki with fruit sauce

Freshly cooked rice

Tofu, wakame and spring onion salad

Creamy tofu cheesecake

SPRING MEAL FOR 4

Grilled bamboo shoot with herb cream

Chicken yakitori

Swordfish teriyaki with fruit sauce

Freshly cooked rice

Green tea chiffon cake

SUMMER MEAL FOR 4

Scallop carpaccio

Japanese-style white meatloaf

Stewed cold aubergines

Summer-style somen noodles

Black sesame ice cream with beetroot chips

AUTUMN MEAL FOR 4

Simmered daikon with chicken sauce

Steamed salmon parcels with vegetables

Freshly cooked rice

Five vegetable pickle

Sweet chestnut dumplings

WINTER MEAL FOR 4

Fried tofu in hot broth

Spicy chicken

Cucumber and seaweed salad

Redbush tea pilaf with walnuts

Baked sweet potato with apple sauce

SEAFOOD MEAL FOR 4

Grilled seafood skewers

Sushi balls with white fish

Miso grilled scorpion fish

Aduki bean and nut pie

VEGETARIAN MEAL FOR 4

Japanese-style vichyssoise (made with
  vegetarian dashi stock)

Stuffed pumpkin

Stir-fried bean sprouts and chilli

Brown rice with mushrooms and
  edamame

Fig cake

MEAT-BASED MEAL FOR 4

Marinated and steamed pork fillet
  (use half the quantity as a starter)

Lotus root and black beans in curry sauce

Steak with rice tubes

Mixed green leaves tossed with sesame oil
  (see Crispy Grilled Liver, page 93)

Ginger and lemon sorbet
  *(make sorbet only from Plum Wine Jelly with
  Ginger and Lemon Sorbet, page 156)*

SUSHI AND SASHIMI DINNER FOR 8

White sashimi salad

Marinated mackerel sushi

Rolled sushi

Sushi with cooked fish topping

Steamed clams in sake

Japanese-style pancake rolls

HOTPOT DINNER FOR 4–6

Marinated fried whitebait

Duck and leek hotpot

Freshly cooked rice

Black sesame ice cream with beetroot chips

BANQUET MENU FOR 10–15

Easy sushi canapés

Grilled vegetables with dips

Fish terrine with green dressing

Grilled prawns in spring rolls

Chicken yakitori
  (make double quantity)

Rice-coated meatballs

Sprouted brown rice sushi in tofu pouches

Creamy tofu cheesecake

Green tea chiffon cake

Seasonal fresh fruits

Basic recipes

White rice
When it is served with other dishes 125–150 g (4–5 oz) per person is sufficient. If a recipe calls for 700 g (1 lb 7 oz) cooked rice use 250 g (8 oz) rice and 325 ml (11 fl oz) water. Sushi and other dishes require different quantities, and these are specified in the relevant recipes. When it is properly cooked, you should be able to see that more than half the rice grains are standing upright and that there are tiny gaps between the grains.

INGREDIENTS *210 g (7¼ oz) Japanese rice or short grain white rice*

ONE Put the rice in a heavy-based saucepan and wash it under cold running water, stirring the rice with your hand. Carefully drain away the water. Repeat, changing the water 2–3 times. Drain well and add 260 ml (8 fl oz) water. Leave to stand for at least 30 minutes or overnight. **TWO** Cover the pan tightly and bring to the boil. Reduce the heat immediately and simmer for 12 minutes or until you hear a faint crackling noise. **THREE** Remove the pan from the heat and leave to stand, covered, for a further 10 minutes. **FOUR** Scoop out the rice with a rice paddle when it is required.

Makes about 600 g (1¼ lb) cooked rice

Brown rice
Brown rice is chewier than white rice, and people tend to feel satisfied by a slightly smaller portion of brown rice than of white.

INGREDIENTS *200 g (7 oz) Japanese brown rice or short grain brown rice*

ONE Follow the method for white rice (see above) but use 500 ml (17 fl oz) water. **TWO** Cook the rice for 40–45 minutes and leave to stand for 10 minutes. Again, listen to the crackling noise and do not lift the lid or stir until the end of the standing time.

Makes about 600 g (1¼ lb) cooked rice

Sushi rice

INGREDIENTS *250 g (8 oz) Japanese rice or short grain rice* ‖ *piece of konbu (kelp), 10 cm (4 inches) square*

SUSHIZU (VINEGAR MIX) *2½ tablespoons rice vinegar* ‖ *1½ tablespoons caster sugar* ‖ *½ teaspoon salt*

ONE Wash the rice as white rice *(see page 17)* but drain it into a sieve and leave for 30 minutes. **TWO** Put the rice in a pan with 325 ml (11 fl oz) water and the konbu and cook as white rice. **THREE** Make the vinegar mix by mixing together all the ingredients in a jug or bowl. **FOUR** Transfer the rice to a large bowl or wooden sushi rice tub. Discard the konbu and drizzle half the vinegar mix over the hot rice. Hold the rice paddle vertically and mix the rice with a cutting motion to avoid squashing the grains. If you have a helper, ask them to fan the hot rice as you mix it so that it cools quickly, which makes it glossy. Pour over the remaining vinegar mix and mix again. **FIVE** Cover the bowl or tub with a wet cloth and leave at room temperature to cool.

Makes about 700 g (1 lb 7 oz) cooked rice

Gari

Ready-made gari (pickled sweet and sour ginger) is available in shops, but it often has a colouring added to make it deep pink. The following recipe doesn't use any colouring, and the resulting pickle is pale pink. If you want a deeper colour, add a slice of red beetroot to the pickling liquid after the pan has been removed from the heat. Remove and discard the beetroot after a few hours. Once made, gari can be kept in the refrigerator for up to 4 weeks.

INGREDIENTS *4½ tablespoons rice vinegar* ‖ *2 tablespoons caster sugar* ‖ *⅔ teaspoon salt* ‖ *200 g (7 oz) fresh root ginger, peeled and finely sliced crossways*

ONE Mix together the vinegar, sugar and salt in a saucepan and bring to the boil. Add the ginger slices and cook for 2 minutes over a moderate heat. **TWO** Remove the saucepan from the heat and leave to cool. **THREE** Transfer the gari to a screw-top jar or plastic container with a lid and leave for the flavours to infuse for 24 hours before using.

Makes 160 g (5¾ oz)

Dashi stock

Although dashi stock is best made fresh every time you need it, leftover stock can be frozen in an ice cube tray; use the cubes within 4 weeks. The liquid that results at the end of step 2 is called *ichiban dashi* or first stock, and it has the more delicate flavour. Use this stock for clear soups or special dishes. The second stock, *niban dashi*, can be used in any dish that requires dashi stock.

INGREDIENTS *piece of konbu (kelp), 5 x 10 cm (2 x 4 inches)* ‖ *30 g (1¼ oz) kezuri bushi (dried bonito)*

ONE Wipe the konbu with damp kitchen paper and make 3–4 slits in it with scissors. Soak it in a pan with 1 litre (1¾ pints) water for 30 minutes. Bring the pan to the boil and remove and reserve the konbu when small bubbles are seen around its edge. **TWO** Return the pan to the boil and add half the kezuri bushi. When the water starts to bubble, remove the pan from the heat. Strain the liquid through a fine sieve or a piece of muslin. (Do not squeeze the liquid out if you use muslin.) **THREE** Pour another 1 litre (1¾ pints) water into the pan and return the konbu and kezuri bushi used for making the first stock. Bring to the boil, then reduce the heat to low and simmer for 20 minutes. **FOUR** Add the remaining kezuri bushi and simmer for another 5 minutes. Remove from the heat and wait for 5 minutes. Strain the liquid through a sieve and use as required.

Makes 2 litres (3½ pints)

Vegetarian dashi stock

This version, which omits the flaked dried bonito, can be used in any dish that requires dashi stock.

INGREDIENTS *piece of konbu (kelp), 10 x 20 cm (4 x 8 inches)*

ONE Wipe the konbu with damp kitchen paper and make 3–4 slits in it with scissors. Soak it in a pan with 1 litre (1¾ pints) water for ½–1 hour. **TWO** Bring the water to the boil and remove the konbu when you can see small bubbles around its edge.

Makes 1 litre (1¾ pints)

Suri goma

Ground roasted sesame seeds, suri goma, can be used in sesame sauce, added to dressings or sprinkled over freshly cooked rice or noodles. It's best to make this fresh every time you need it because the aroma of the sesame oil evaporates within a day.

INGREDIENTS *1 tablespoon white or black roasted sesame seeds*

ONE Thoroughly wash and dry a surikogi and suribachi (pestle and mortar). **TWO** Grind the roasted sesame seeds in the mortar with a circular motion. **THREE** After about 5 minutes the crushed sesame seeds will start to release their oil. Continue to grind until a moist but crumbly paste appears, which may take about 15 minutes.

Makes 1½ teaspoons

Tsuyu, recipe A

This type of tsuyu is used as a soup to accompany noodles.

INGREDIENTS *1½ tablespoons mirin* ‖ *1½ tablespoons shoyu* ‖ *1 teaspoon salt* ‖ *20 g (¾ oz) kezuri bushi (dried bonito flakes)* ‖ *piece of konbu (kelp), 5 x 10 cm (2 x 4 inches)*

ONE Pour the mirin into a large saucepan. Bring to the boil for 10 seconds then add the shoyu, salt and 1 litre (1¾ pints) water. Wait a second and add the kezuri bushi and konbu. Let the mixture bubble for 2 minutes without stirring. **TWO** Remove the saucepan from the heat and strain the mixture through a muslin cloth into a bowl. Lift the cloth but do not squeeze it and wait until all the liquid has drained. Reheat as required.

Makes enough soup for 4

Tsuyu, recipe B

Make this recipe when you need a dipping sauce to accompany noodles. Use it at room temperature with your choice of condiments.

INGREDIENTS *100 ml (3½ fl oz) mirin ‖ 100 ml (3½ fl oz) shoyu ‖ 20 g (¾ oz) kezuri bushi (dried bonito)*

ONE Pour the mirin into a large saucepan, bring it to the boil for 10 seconds then reduce the heat to low. Add the shoyu and kezuri bushi. Shake the pan instead of stirring to mix the ingredients. **TWO** Add 400 ml (14 fl oz) water and return to the boil. Let the sauce bubble for 3–4 minutes, then remove it from the heat and strain through a muslin cloth as for Tsuyu, recipe A.

Makes enough dipping sauce for 4

Beni shoga

Beni shoga (pickled ginger) can vary in colour from pale pink to deep red depending on whether the umesu (plum vinegar) used contains red shiso or not. Once made, the pickle can be kept in the refrigerator for up to 4 weeks, and after 2 days it will be ready to use as a condiment to meat, fish or noodle dishes. Remove the apple after 2 days if the alternative pickling liquid is used. Umesu is sold in health shops in many European countries and the USA.

INGREDIENTS *250 g (8 oz) fresh root ginger, peeled ‖ 20 g (¾ oz) coarse sea salt ‖ 1 tablespoon rice vinegar ‖ 250 ml (8 fl oz) umesu (plum vinegar)*

ALTERNATIVE PICKLING LIQUID *250 ml (8 fl oz) cider vinegar ‖ 1 tablespoon salt ‖ 1 apple, quartered*

ONE Put the ginger, salt and vinegar into a watertight plastic bag. Leave to infuse in the refrigerator for a week. **TWO** Wipe the salt and excess liquid from the ginger with kitchen paper and cut it into matchsticks using a sharp knife or mandolin (a cheese grater makes the sections too rough). **THREE** Put the ginger in a screw-top jar and pour in the umesu or the vinegar, salt and apple pieces.

Makes 450 g (1 lb)

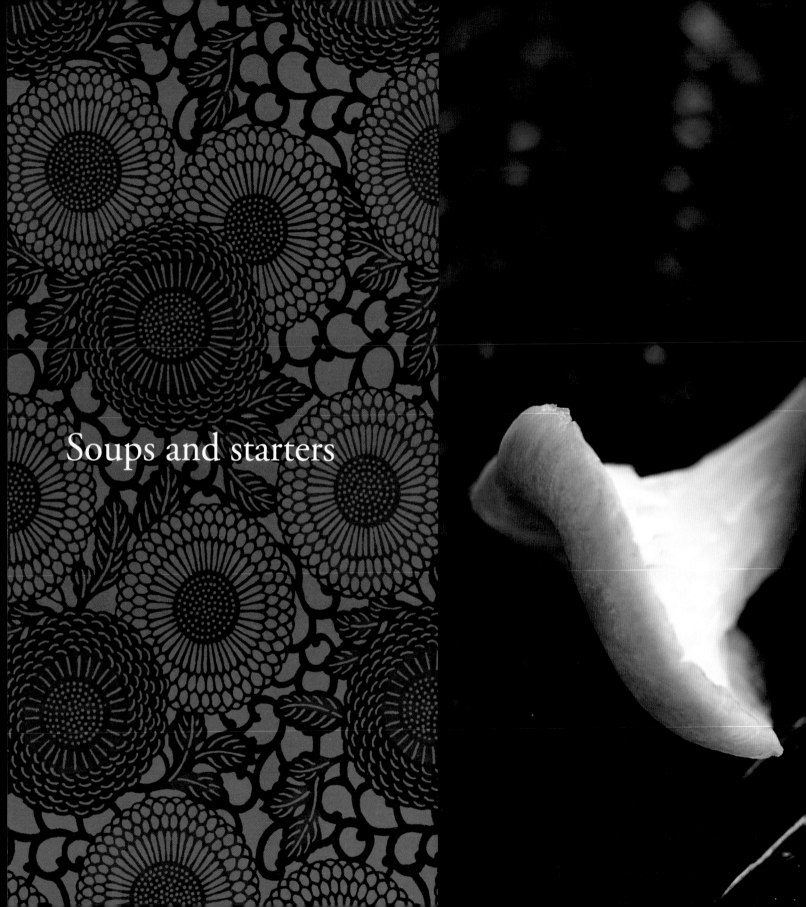

Soups and starters

Clear soup with prawns

Ebi no o-suimono This soup is often served at celebratory meals, such as at weddings and on New Year's Day. It is normally accompanied by rice and other dishes. Mitsuba resembles flat leaf parsley but has a more aromatic, delicate flavour.

INGREDIENTS *4 small, uncooked tiger prawns with the heads on* ‖ *2 tablespoons sake or dry sherry* ‖ *20 g (¾ oz) daikon, peeled and cut into 4 slices* ‖ *20 g (¾ oz) carrot, cut into 4 slices* ‖ *600 ml (1 pint) Dashi Stock (see page 19)* ‖ *1 teaspoon shoyu* ‖ *⅓ teaspoon salt*

TO GARNISH *1 bunch of mitsuba (Japanese parsley) or chives, blanched* ‖ *rind of ¼ lemon*

ONE Place the prawns in a saucepan and pour over 1 tablespoon sake mixed with 1 tablespoon water. Cook the prawns over a medium heat until the shells turn red. Remove them from the pan and leave to cool. Remove the shells but leave on the heads and tails. **TWO** Put the daikon and carrot into another pan and pour over enough cold water to cover. Bring to the boil, cook for 3 minutes, then drain. **THREE** Bring the stock to the boil and add the shoyu, the remaining sake and the salt. **FOUR** Spoon the vegetables into 4 soup bowls. Put a prawn in each, then pour over the hot soup. Garnish with mitsuba leaves and lemon rind and serve immediately.

Serves 4

NUTRIENT ANALYSIS PER SERVING 72 kJ – 17 cal – 1 g protein – 1 g carbohydrate – 0.5 g sugars – 0 g fat – 0 g saturated fat – 0 g fibre – 320 mg sodium

HEALTHY TIP Fat is the most concentrated source of calories we eat. This tasty soup is fat free, and therefore very low in calories.

Egg soup *Kakitama jiru* The eggs float gracefully, like pale yellow flowers, on the surface of this simple soup, which is thickened with arrowroot. It is an elegant but quick to make soup, which is served at home in Japan. The shoots of green and dwarf beans are sometimes available for salads and stir-fries in farmers' markets and specialist greengrocers.

INGREDIENTS *1 litre (1¾ pints) Dashi Stock (see page 19)* ‖ *1 teaspoon salt* ‖ *1 teaspoon arrowroot or cornflour* ‖ *4 eggs, beaten* ‖ *100 g (3½ oz) bean shoot leaves or lamb's lettuce* ‖ *1 teaspoon juice from about 5 cm (2 inches) fresh root ginger, peeled, grated and squeezed*

ONE Put the stock in a saucepan, bring it to the boil and add the salt. Mix the arrowroot with 1 teaspoon water, add to the stock and stir well. **TWO** Reduce the heat to moderate and leave, uncovered, for 1–2 minutes or until the soup has thickened. There is no need to stir. **THREE** Stir the soup to create a whirlpool and slowly pour in the eggs. Cook for 2 minutes or until the eggs have set in the soup. **FOUR** Add the bean shoot leaves and ginger juice, stir to mix and serve immediately.

Serves 4

NUTRIENT ANALYSIS PER SERVING 370 kJ – 89 cal – 7 g protein – 2 g carbohydrate – 0 g sugars – 6 g fat – 2 g saturated fat – 0 g fibre – 630 mg sodium

HEALTHY TIP Eggs are a very good source of protein, and the yolk provides iron and vitamins A and D.

Japanese-style vichyssoise *Tonyu hiyashi-jiru*

By mid-morning at the height of the Japanese summer the temperature and humidity can rise to almost unbearable levels. Cold soups like this are not only thirst quenching and cooling but also a good way to maintain nutrition levels when the weather causes everyone to lose their appetite.

INGREDIENTS *1 tablespoon vegetable oil* ‖ *1 garlic clove, crushed* ‖ *½ onion, chopped roughly* ‖ *400 g (13 oz) potatoes, cut into slices 5 mm (¼ inch) thick* ‖ *200 ml (7 fl oz) Dashi Stock (see page 19)* ‖ *1 dried bay leaf* ‖ *300 ml (½ pint) unsweetened soya milk* ‖ *1 tablespoon white or yellow miso* ‖ *a few chives, finely chopped, to garnish*

ONE Heat the oil in a medium-sized, nonstick pan and fry the garlic until is just softened. Add the onion and potatoes and fry for 3 minutes. **TWO** Add the stock and bay leaf to the pan, cover and cook over a low heat until the potatoes are soft. **THREE** Transfer the mixture to a food processor and add the soya milk and miso. Liquidize until the soup is smooth, allow to cool and then transfer to the refrigerator. Serve cold, sprinkled with the chives.

Serves 4

NUTRIENT ANALYSIS PER SERVING 580 kJ – 138 cal – 5 g protein – 20 g carbohydrate – 2 g sugars – 5 g fat – 1 g saturated fat – 2 g fibre – 180 mg sodium

HEALTHY TIP The vitamin C content of potatoes is close to the skin, so peel your potatoes as thinly as possible to preserve the vitamin content.

Fried tofu in hot broth

Agedashi tofu The tofu is deep-fried, but most of the oil is washed away in the clear broth. The crispy coat around the tofu, soaked in delicate dashi broth, makes this dish rich and satisfying. Although silken tofu is preferred, you can use firm tofu if necessary. To make a light-coloured broth use *usukuchi shoyu* (pale tofu).

INGREDIENTS *280 g (9½ oz) silken tofu* ‖ *500 g (1 lb) daikon, peeled* ‖ *5 cm (2 inches) fresh root ginger, peeled and grated* ‖ *4 tablespoons arrowroot or cornflour* ‖ *pinch of salt* ‖ *vegetable oil, for frying* ‖ *1 spring onion (green part only), finely chopped*

BROTH *200 ml (7 fl oz) Dashi Stock (see page 19)* ‖ *50 ml (2 fl oz) shoyu* ‖ *50 ml (2 fl oz) mirin* ‖ *1½ tablespoons sake*

ONE Wrap the tofu in a clean tea towel, place a chopping board or other weight on top and leave to remove the excess water. This will take about 30 minutes, and you should change the tea towel once. Alternatively, put the tofu in a microwave and heat for 1 minute (on 700W). Cut the tofu into 5 cm (2 inch) cubes. **TWO** Make the broth by mixing together all the ingredients in a heavy-based saucepan. Heat but do not boil and keep warm. **THREE** Use a Japanese grater to grate the daikon. Squeeze and discard the juice from the daikon and form the flesh into 4 conical mounds. Add one-quarter of the grated ginger on top of each. **FOUR** Mix together the arrowroot and salt and dust the tofu cubes with the mixture. Add oil to a large, nonstick frying pan to a depth of about 2.5 cm (1 inch) and heat it to 170°C (340°F). Fry the tofu until the outsides are golden and crisp and drain on kitchen paper. **FIVE** Divide the tofu among 4 bowls, top each with a daikon mound and some spring onion. Pour hot broth into each bowl and serve immediately.

Serves 4

NUTRIENT ANALYSIS PER SERVING 1037 kJ – 247 cal – 8 g protein – 32 g carbohydrate – 1 g sugars – 9 g fat – 1 g saturated fat – 0 g fibre – 770 mg sodium

HEALTHY TIP Tofu is a good source of protein, and is also high in calcium, important for growth and maintenance of bones. It does not contain the growth hormone oestrogen – as believed by some – which is only produced by animals.

Simmered daikon with chicken sauce *Furohuki daikon*

tori soboro kake Slow-cooked daikon is a traditional Japanese vegetable dish. Here it is updated with a white meat sauce and crispy filo crust. Choose a daikon with a thick part about 20 cm (8 inches) long.

INGREDIENTS *piece of konbu (kelp), 2.5 cm (1 inch) square* ‖ *1 large daikon, thickly peeled and cut into 5 cm (2 inch) wedges* ‖ *1 tablespoon uncooked white rice* ‖ *100 ml (3½ fl oz) sake* ‖ *200 g (7 oz) boneless, skinless chicken thigh, minced* ‖ *5 cm (2 inches) fresh root ginger, peeled and finely chopped* ‖ *100 ml (3½ fl oz) white or yellow miso* ‖ *50 g (2 oz) walnuts, finely chopped* ‖ *2 sheets of filo pastry, each about 30 cm (12 inches) square* ‖ *2 teaspoons mayonnaise* ‖ *1 teaspoon milk* ‖ *½ sheet of nori, cut into thin strips*

ONE Place the konbu in a heavy-based saucepan and put the daikon on top. Cover with water, add the rice and bring to the boil. Immediately reduce the heat and simmer, uncovered, for 30 minutes. Use a skewer to check that the daikon is thoroughly cooked, then leave to cool. **TWO** Put the sake in another saucepan and bring to the boil. Add the chicken and ginger and cook, stirring, over a moderate heat. When the liquid has almost evaporated add the miso and walnuts and stir well to mix. **THREE** Fold the filo pastry to make 16 small squares. The filo squares should be larger than the pieces of daikon. Mix together the mayonnaise and milk and brush each filo square with the mixture. Sprinkle over the nori strips and layer a few filo squares on top of each other. Transfer them to a lightly oiled baking sheet, cook under a hot grill until crisp and leave to cool. **FOUR** Transfer the daikon to 4 plates and top with the meat sauce. Garnish with the crispy filo squares and serve immediately.

Serves 4

NUTRIENT ANALYSIS PER SERVING 1490 kJ – 358 cal – 18 g protein – 25 g carbohydrate – 1 g sugars – 18 g fat – 2 g saturated fat – 1 g fibre – 1145 mg sodium

HEALTHY TIP Using a reduced fat (light) mayonnaise will lower the fat, and therefore calorie content of this dish.

Grilled vegetables with tofu mayonnaise *Yaki yasai*

moriawase The low-calorie tofu mayonnaise that accompanies the vegetables has a subtler taste than the ordinary egg-and-oil version, and it perfectly compliments the crunchy vegetables.

INGREDIENTS *1 large sweet potato, cut into 5 mm (¼ inch) slices* ‖ *125 g (4 oz) maitake mushroom, torn into strips* ‖ *2 long, slim aubergines or 1 round aubergine, cut into 5 mm (¼ inch) slices* ‖ *16 baby courgettes, halved lengthways* ‖ *1 tablespoon walnut oil* ‖ *½ teaspoon salt* ‖ *1 garlic bulb* ‖ *16 kumquats, halved* ‖ *cracked black pepper (optional), to serve*

TOFU MAYONNAISE *125 g (4 oz) tofu* ‖ *4 tablespoons walnut oil* ‖ *4 tablespoons rice vinegar* ‖ *⅓ teaspoon salt* ‖ *½ teaspoon mustard powder*

ONE Make the mayonnaise. Drain the tofu and wrap it in kitchen paper for 30 minutes. Blend the tofu with the oil, vinegar, salt and mustard powder in a food processor until smooth, then transfer to the refrigerator until needed. **TWO** Put the sweet potato, mushroom, aubergines and courgettes in a large plastic bag. Add the walnut oil and salt and turn the vegetables in the bag so that they are lightly coated in oil. **THREE** Separate the garlic bulb into cloves but leave on the skins. Cook all the vegetables and the kumquats in a griddle or over a barbecue. Alternatively, bake them in a preheated oven, 230°C (450°F), Gas Mark 8; the sweet potatoes will take about 30 minutes to cook, and the remaining vegetables will require 10–15 minutes. **FOUR** Squeeze out the cooked garlic from its skin. Serve all the vegetables and kumquats on a large plate with cracked black pepper (if used) and accompanied by a small bowl of the mayonnaise to dip.

Serves 4

NUTRIENT ANALYSIS PER SERVING 1344 kJ – 320 cal – 8 g protein – 37 g carbohydrate – 16 g sugars – 17 g fat – 2 g saturated fat – 5 g fibre – 320 mg sodium

HEALTHY TIP Walnut oil is high in polyunsaturated fatty acids, which help to protect against coronary heart disease and possibly some forms of cancer.

Chicken yakitori

Yakitori This dish is often mistaken for a similar dish from Southeast Asia, but Japanese yakitori is not eaten with peanut sauce. The chicken is either barbecued with a tangy, shoyu-based sauce or plainly grilled with just a sprinkling of salt and lemon.

INGREDIENTS *500 g (1 lb) chicken thighs (with skin), cut into 48 pieces* ‖ *2 tablespoons sake* ‖ *12 spring onions, cut into 2.5 cm (1 inch) pieces* ‖ *16 shishitou sweet chilli peppers (optional)* ‖ *shichimi togarashi, to serve*

TERIYAKI SAUCE *3 tablespoons shoyu* ‖ *2 tablespoons mirin* ‖ *1 tablespoon sake* ‖ *juice from 2.5 cm (1 inch) fresh root ginger, peeled, grated and squeezed*

ONE Soak 20 bamboo skewers in water overnight. Make the teriyaki sauce. Mix together the shoyu, mirin and sake in a saucepan and bring to the boil for 20 seconds. Reduce the heat to low and simmer for 15 minutes. Add the ginger juice and stir. Remove the saucepan from the heat. The liquid should be reduced by one-third and be slightly sticky. Transfer the sauce to a screw-top jar. It can be stored in the refrigerator for up to a week. **TWO** Put the chicken in a large plastic bag and add the sake. Turn over the chicken until it is coated in sake and leave to marinate for an hour in the refrigerator. **THREE** Thread 3 pieces of chicken and some spring onion on to each of 16 skewers. Thread 4 chillies (if used) on to each of the 4 remaining skewers and set aside. **FOUR** Cook the skewers under a preheated hot grill for 15–25 minutes, turning and brushing with about 6 tablespoons teriyaki sauce as they cook. Alternatively, cook the skewers on a lightly oiled griddle over a charcoal fire, turning and cooking as above. Serve hot with shichimi togarashi.

Makes 16–20 skewers; serves 4

NUTRIENT ANALYSIS PER SERVING 837 kJ – 200 cal – 17 g protein – 2 g carbohydrate – 1 g sugars – 12 g fat – 3 g saturated fat – 0 g fibre – 716 mg sodium

HEALTHY TIP Leaving the skin on the chicken keeps the flesh moist, but if you want to reduce the calories in this dish remove the skin before eating.

Miso soup with pork and vegetables

Tonjiru Slightly sticky satoimo (potato), chewy pieces of pork and chunks of silky tofu provide a medley of textures to enjoy with this filling soup. Some types of miso are saltier than others, so adjust the amount you add to taste. You could use unsmoked bacon instead of pork. For a light lunch serve this dish with a bowl of freshly cooked rice and some pickles.

INGREDIENTS *200 g (7 oz) satoimo, taro or yam* ‖ *1 teaspoon sesame oil* ‖ *200 g (7 oz) pork belly or leg, thinly sliced* ‖ *100 g (3½ oz) daikon, peeled, thickly sliced and cut into quarters* ‖ *1 thick carrot, thickly sliced and cut into thick quarters* ‖ *100 g (3½ oz) atsuage (deep-fried thick tofu)* ‖ *1 litre (1¾ pints) Dashi Stock (see page 19)* ‖ *4–6 tablespoons red or brown miso* ‖ *2 spring onions, finely chopped* ‖ *shichimi togarashi, to serve*

ONE Peel the satoimo and rinse it in water. Parboil for 5 minutes, then drain and rinse away the sticky juice. Cut it into semicircles 8 mm (⅓ inch) thick. **TWO** Heat the sesame oil in a heavy-based saucepan and fry the pork over a high heat for 2 minutes. Add the daikon, carrot and atsuage and cook, stirring, for 3 minutes. **THREE** Add the stock and bring to the boil. Reduce the heat and simmer for 5 minutes or until all the vegetables are cooked but are not too soft. **FOUR** Stir in miso to taste. Sprinkle over the spring onions and serve the soup hot with shichimi togarashi.

Serves 4

NUTRIENT ANALYSIS PER SERVING

994 kJ – 236 cal – 19 g protein – 19 g carbohydrate – 3 g sugars – 10 g fat – 2 g saturated fat – 4 g fibre – 917 mg sodium

HEALTHY TIP The vegetables in this soup are a good source of dietary fibre, which helps to ensure a healthy bowel, and protect against bowel cancer.

Fish terrine with green dressing *Sakana no terinu* White fish and

scallops are combined to make a smooth and creamy terrine. If possible, use a Japanese grater to grate the

daikon for the dressing because it retains the nutritious juice.

INGREDIENTS *14 green and 10 white asparagus spears, trimmed and lightly boiled*

TERRINE *180 g (6¼ oz) sole or flounder fillet, skinned* ‖ *180 g (6¼ oz) scallops, coral removed* ‖ *2 eggs,
beaten* ‖ *270 ml (9 fl oz) crème fraîche* ‖ *1 teaspoon brandy* ‖ *½ teaspoon salt, to taste*

DRESSING *3 tablespoons lemon juice* ‖ *4½ tablespoons olive oil, plus extra for greasing* ‖ *½ teaspoon salt* ‖
30 g (1¼ oz) daikon, grated

ONE Make the terrine by blending together all the ingredients (except the salt) in a food processor. Add salt to taste. **TWO** Lightly oil a 1.2 litre (2 pint) terrine mould and pour in one-quarter of the mixture. Reserve 4 green asparagus spears for the dressing and arrange about one-third of the remaining spears over the terrine. Cover with more terrine mixture. Repeat the layers to fill the mould. Cover with clingfilm. **THREE** Transfer the terrine to a steamer and cook over a moderate to low heat for 30 minutes. Alternatively, place the terrine in a baking pan, half-filled with boiling water, and cook in a preheated oven, 180°C (350°F), Gas Mark 4, for 45–60 minutes. Leave to cool. **FOUR** Purée the reserved asparagus spears and sieve into a bowl. Add the ingredients for the dressing to the puréed asparagus and mix together. **FIVE** Carefully slice the cold terrine and serve with the dressing.

Serves 6–8

NUTRIENT ANALYSIS PER SERVING 1486 kJ – 359 cal – 17 g protein – 4 g carbohydrate – 3 g sugars – 30 g fat – 14 g saturated fat – 1 g fibre – 434 mg sodium

HEALTHY TIP Olive oil is a good source of mono-unsaturated fatty acids, which are thought to protect against coronary heart disease.

Steamed savoury pudding

Chawan mushi In Japan this dish replaces the soup course, making a good starter for a dinner on a cold autumn or winter day. The savoury egg mixture is steamed gently to form a smooth set custard, with little treasures, such as a piece of prawn or ginkgo nut, hidden inside.

INGREDIENTS *1 teaspoon shoyu* ‖ *100 g (3½ oz) skinless chicken breast, cut into bite-sized pieces* ‖ *3 eggs, beaten* ‖ *500 ml (17 fl oz) Dashi Stock (see page 19)* ‖ *1 teaspoon salt* ‖ *12 shelled ginkgo nuts (fresh or canned)* ‖ *50 g (2 oz) shimeji mushrooms, trimmed* ‖ *12 cooked prawns* ‖ *8 mangetout, blanched in salted water*

ONE Sprinkle ½ teaspoon shoyu over the chicken and leave it to stand for 10 minutes. **TWO** Meanwhile, mix the eggs with the stock in a bowl and stir in the salt and remaining shoyu. Strain the mixture into a large jug. **THREE** Divide the ginkgo nuts, mushrooms, chicken and prawns among 4 individual bowls, tea cups or ramekins. **FOUR** Heat plenty of water in a large steamer and put the cups into the steamer. Carefully pour in the egg mixture. Cover the steamer with a tea towel and put on the lid. Steam over high heat for 2 minutes, then reduce the heat to the lowest setting for another 10 minutes. Alternatively, use a heavy-based saucepan and line the base with a tea towel. Add 2.5 cm (1 inch) of water and bring it to the boil. Cover each bowl with clingfilm and carefully place them in the pan. Cover and cook as for the steamer method. **FIVE** Check that the pudding is set by inserting a toothpick into the centre: if it remains standing, the custard is ready. Garnish with mangetout and serve hot.

Serves 4

NUTRIENT ANALYSIS PER SERVING 520 kJ – 124 cal – 14 g protein – 1 g carbohydrate – 0 g sugars – 7 g fat – 2 g saturated fat – 1 g fibre – 820 mg sodium

HEALTHY TIP Proteins are made up of amino acids, and the protein in eggs has a high content of the so-called essential amino acids, which cannot be made in the body.

Sushi and sashimi

Hand-rolled sushi

Temaki-zushi Temaki sushi is like a self-service sandwich bar. Try a variety of fillings, ranging from the usual sushi ingredients to anything that is suitable for a sandwich, such as smoked salmon, cheese, ham and roast beef or chicken.

INGREDIENTS *400 g (13 oz) of at least 3 types of fresh fish fillets and shellfish, such as tuna, yellowtail, salmon, bream, mackerel, squid bodies and large cooked prawns* ‖ *1 avocado, peeled and stoned* ‖ *2 teaspoons lemon juice* ‖ *½ cucumber, cut into 5 mm x 8 cm (¼ x 3 inch) sticks* ‖ *2 spring onions, cut in half, then into thin strips* ‖ *4 shiso leaves, cut into thin strips* ‖ *600 g (1¼ lb) freshly cooked sushi rice (see page 18)* ‖ *10 sheets of nori* ‖ *4 plain tortillas*

TO SERVE *mayonnaise* ‖ *wasabi (optional)* ‖ *shoyu* ‖ *gari (see page 18)*

ONE Prepare the fillings. Remove the skin from the fish and cut the flesh into 1 x 3 cm (½ x 3 inch) strips, slicing across the grain as much as possible. If you are using mackerel prepare the fillet as described for Marinated Mackerel Sushi *(see page 48)*. Cut the flesh into the same size strips as the other fish. **TWO** Cut the avocado flesh into slices 5 mm (¼ inch) thick and sprinkle over the lemon juice. Arrange all the sushi ingredients on a large serving tray and keep in the refrigerator until you are ready to serve. **THREE** Put the sushi rice in a large bowl. Give each guest 2 small plates, 1 for the rolled sushi and the other for the shoyu dip. Just before serving cut each nori sheet and tortilla into 4 pieces. **FOUR** To eat, put a piece of nori or tortilla on a plate and spread it with 1–2 tablespoons rice, adding a smear of mayonnaise or wasabi if a hot, spicy taste is preferred. Lay 2–3 fillings, such as tuna and shiso leaves or cucumber and salmon, diagonally over the rice. Roll the nori or tortilla around the filling to give a conical shape (as if wrapping a bouquet of flowers). Guests should dip the sushi into shoyu and eat a roll as they complete it, nibbling some gari between the rolls to clean their palates.

Serves 4–6

NUTRIENT ANALYSIS PER SERVING 2077 kJ – 493 cal – 33 g protein – 70 g carbohydrate – 5 g sugars – 11 g fat – 2 g saturated fat – 3 g fibre – 1260 mg sodium

HEALTHY TIP Mackerel has a high fat content which is an excellent source of omega-3 fatty acids.

Marinated tuna sashimi

Maguro butsu Ask your fishmonger if the tuna is fresh enough to eat raw. It's best to avoid the prepacked tuna sometimes available in supermarkets, because it is difficult to check its freshness. Sashimi can be eaten as a starter or as a main dish with a bowl of rice and other small dishes. All the ingredients must be kept cold until they are served.

INGREDIENTS *½–3 teaspoons wasabi* ‖ *3 tablespoons shoyu* ‖ *450 g (14½ oz) fresh tuna steak, cut into 2 cm (¾ inch) cubes* ‖ *½ sheet of nori, cut into thin strips* ‖ *½ large cucumber, cut into matchsticks* ‖ *1 pack of salad cress* ‖ *4 shiso leaves, cut into thin strips*

ONE Put the wasabi in a bowl and add the shoyu, stirring thoroughly to mix. Add the tuna and leave to marinate for 5 minutes. Add the strips of nori. **TWO** Squeeze the liquid from the cucumber and mix together the cress, cucumber and shiso leaves. Divide among 4 plates or small bowls, place the tuna on top of the vegetables and serve immediately.

Serves 4 as a starter

NUTRIENT ANALYSIS PER SERVING 710 kJ – 169 cal – 29 g protein – 2 g carbohydrate – 1 g sugars – 5 g fat – 1 g saturated fat – 1 g fibre – 927 mg sodium

HEALTHY TIP Although tuna may be classified as a fatty fish, the fat content is not very high and is mostly polyunsaturated fatty acids. Tuna is a good source of protein.

Rolled sushi

Hosomaki Before you begin, add 1 tablespoon rice vinegar to 500 ml (17 fl oz) water to make a *tezu* in which you can dampen your fingers.

INGREDIENTS *4 sheets of nori, cut in half* ‖ *600 g (1¼ lb) freshly made sushi rice (see page 17)* ‖ *½ takuan (pickled daikon), about 10 cm (4 inches) long, cut into 1 cm (½ inch) strips* ‖ *½ bunch of chives* ‖ *8 shiso leaves, cut in half lengthways* ‖ *250 g (8 oz) tuna fillet, cut lengthways into 1 cm (½ inch) strips* ‖ *2 tablespoons roasted white sesame seeds*

TO SERVE *gari (see page 18)* ‖ *shoyu* ‖ *1 tablespoon wasabi (optional)*

ONE Put the rolling mat on the work surface with the bamboo horizontally towards you. Lay a piece of nori, shiny side down, on the mat with the edge of the nori against the edge of the mat nearest to you. Place 75 g (3 oz) rice on the nori, dampen your fingertips and spread the rice over the nori, leaving 5 mm (¼ inch) free at the end. Draw a horizontal groove along the centre of the rice with your finger and put a quarter of the takuan and chives in the space. **TWO** Lift and hold the nearest edge of the mat, keeping the filling in place with your fourth fingers. Roll up the mat until its nearest edge touches the clear space at the top. Grip the mat with both hands, tighten the roll and lift the mat slightly from the sushi. Continue to roll to the end of the mat. Repeat to make 4 rolls. **THREE** Cover the mat with clingfilm. Put a piece of nori on the mat and spread rice over it. Turn it upside down so that it is rice side down. **FOUR** Place shiso leaves 2.5 cm (1 inch) from the front edge, lay tuna pieces on top and roll up to make an inside-out roll. Repeat to make 4 rolls. Coat the outside with sesame seeds. **FIVE** Cut each roll into 6 pieces and serve with gari. Dip into shoyu to eat, adding wasabi, if liked.

Makes 48 pieces; serves 4

NUTRIENT ANALYSIS PER SERVING 1373 kJ – 326 cal – 22 g protein – 46 g carbohydrate – 4 g sugars – 7 g fat – 1 g saturated fat – 2 g fibre – 667 mg sodium

HEALTHY TIP The combination of high protein tuna and starchy rice increases the nutritional value of both foods.

Scallop carpaccio *Hotate sashimi* Melt-in-the-mouth, fresh, raw scallops tingle the tastebuds. Use the coral from the scallops in a stir-fry.

INGREDIENTS *125 g (4 oz) green grapes, peeled and deseeded ‖ 8 scallops, cut into 3–4 slices ‖ 1 tablespoon vegetable oil ‖ 50 g (2 oz) roasted flaked almonds ‖ 60 g (2¼ oz) raspberries, puréed (thawed if frozen) ‖ 2 tablespoons chopped chives*

DRESSING *6 tablespoons raspberry vinegar ‖ 1 tablespoon sake ‖ 4 tablespoons vegetable oil ‖ ⅛ onion, grated or finely chopped ‖ 1 teaspoon honey ‖ ½ teaspoon ground white peppercorns ‖ 1 teaspoon salt*

ONE Make the dressing by mixing together all the ingredients. **TWO** Chop the grapes roughly and mix them with 1 tablespoon of the dressing. Transfer the dressing and the grapes to the refrigerator. **THREE** Arrange the scallop slices on 4 chilled plates and brush them with the oil. **FOUR** Garnish the scallops with the grapes and raspberry purée and sprinkle over the flaked almonds and chives. Pour over the dressing and serve immediately.

Serves 4 as a starter

NUTRIENT ANALYSIS PER SERVING 1228 kJ – 295 cal – 15 g protein – 10 g carbohydrate – 8 g sugars – 22 g fat – 2 g saturated fat – 3 g fibre – 584 mg sodium

HEALTHY TIP All oils are concentrated sources of fat and similar in calorie content, but the fatty acid content varies according to source. Safflower, walnut and sunflower oils have a particularly high polyunsaturated fat content; corn oil is a bit lower, then vegetable oil.

Marinated mackerel sushi *Saba zushi* In this dish the mackerel is

'cooked' in salt and vinegar before being used to top the sushi rice. The fat, dense fish and fresh-tasting rice complement each other perfectly. Edible chrysanthemum leaves (not from the chrysanthemums in your garden) and the petals are available in oriental stores. You can use nasturtium instead of chrysanthemum petals if you prefer.

INGREDIENTS *1 large mackerel, filleted* ‖ *2 tablespoons salt, plus extra for blanching* ‖ *200 ml (7 fl oz) rice vinegar* ‖ *125 g (4 oz) shungiku (edible chrysanthemum leaves) or rocket leaves* ‖ *petals from 1–2 edible chrysanthemum flowers (optional)* ‖ *600 g (1¼ lb) freshly made sushi rice (see page 18)* ‖ *100 g (3½ oz) gari (see page 18),* **to serve**

ONE Use tweezers to remove any bones from the mackerel. Sprinkle salt thickly over the fish and leave it for 2 hours. Wash off the salt and marinate in rice vinegar for 20 minutes. Pat the fish dry on kitchen paper. **TWO** Blanch the chrysanthemum leaves and petals (if used) in lightly salted water for 10 seconds. Drain and squeeze them to remove excess water, then mix them into the rice. **THREE** Lay a piece of clingfilm that is larger than the rolling mat over the mat and place a piece of mackerel on it, skin side down. Spread half the rice over the mackerel. Wrap the mackerel and rice in the clingfilm and twist the ends together. Roll up the mat to make a firm cylinder. Grip the mat with both hands and press the roll on a flat surface to make the base flat. Repeat with the remaining fish and rice to make 2 rolls and leave them at room temperature for between 30 minutes and 3 hours. **FOUR** Remove the clingfilm and cut each roll into 6 pieces, wiping the knife after each cut. Serve with gari.

Serves 4

NUTRIENT ANALYSIS PER SERVING 1480 kJ – 353 cal – 16 g protein – 50 g carbohydrate – 8 g sugars – 11 g fat – 2 g saturated fat – 2 g fibre – 1400 mg sodium

HEALTHY TIP Mackerel is a high fat fish, a good source of the fat-soluble vitamins A and D, and of omega-3 fatty acids. Be sure to wash the salt off the mackerel very thoroughly to reduce the high salt content of the dish.

Yellowtail sashimi with peach sauce

Hamachi sashi This visually extravagant dish is a treat for your palate as well your eyes. Make it for a special dinner party. If you cannot find yellowtail use fresh swordfish or the fatty part of tuna. Juniper berries are available in specialist stores, but you could sprinkle the fish with 1 teaspoon gin while it is marinating instead.

INGREDIENTS *6 teaspoons shoyu* ‖ *1½ teaspoons kurosu (black rice vinegar) or balsamic vinegar* ‖ *300 g (10 oz) fresh hamachi yellowtail fillet, skinned* ‖ *1 sheet of nori, cut in half*

PEACH SAUCE *2 white or yellow peaches, about 200 g (7 oz) in total, peeled and stoned* ‖ *rind of lime, cut into thin strips* ‖ *juice of lime* ‖ *2 tablespoons crème fraîche* ‖ *50 ml (2 fl oz) semi-skimmed milk* ‖ *pinch of salt* ‖ *pinch of white pepper*

TO GARNISH *1 endive, cut into 5 mm (¼ inch) slices* ‖ *15 juniper berries*

ONE Mix together 4 teaspoons shoyu and the vinegar in a non-metallic container, add the fish and leave to marinate for 3 hours in the refrigerator, turning the fish occasionally. **TWO** Meanwhile, make the peach sauce by blending together the ingredients in a food processor to make a smooth purée. **THREE** Wipe any marinade from the fish. Brush the nori with 2 teaspoons shoyu and place the nori on the skin side of the fish. Return the fish to the refrigerator for 10 minutes. **FOUR** Use a sharp knife and cut across the grain to slice the fish into pieces 3 mm (⅛ inch) thick. Arrange these like the spokes of a wheel on 4 plates. **FIVE** Garnish the fish with the endive slices and arrange juniper berries in the centre of the plates. Serve with the peach sauce.

Serves 4 as a starter

NUTRIENT ANALYSIS PER SERVING 665 kJ – 159 cal –16 g protein – 6 g carbohydrate – 5 g sugars – 8 g fat – 4 g saturated fat – 1 g fibre – 540 mg sodium

HEALTHY TIP The fat content of this dish is not very high if low fat (white) fish is used, but it could be reduced more by using half-fat crème fraîche.

Sushi balls with white fish *Shiromi uo no temari-zushi* You could

use smoked halibut instead of white fish. You can use fresh or boiled renkon (lotus root).

INGREDIENTS *2 sheets of dried konbu (kelp), each 10 x 5 cm (4 x 2 inches)* ‖ *100 g (3½ oz) fresh white fish, such as sole, halibut or snapper, filleted and skinned* ‖ *5 cm (2 inches) renkon (lotus root), pre-cooked* ‖ *1 tablespoon rice vinegar* ‖ *½ teaspoon red food colouring* ‖ *700 g (1 lb 7 oz) freshly cooked sushi rice (see page 18)* ‖ *1 tablespoon roasted sesame seeds* ‖ *2 teaspoons wasabi (optional)* ‖ *5 chives, blanched and cut into 3 cm (1¼ inch) lengths* ‖ *shoyu, to serve*

ONE Wipe the konbu with damp kitchen paper and sandwich the fish between the konbu. Wrap the parcel tightly in clingfilm and leave for 2 hours in the refrigerator. Discard the konbu and slice the fish thinly, cutting diagonally across the flesh. **TWO** Add about 800 ml (28 fl oz) water and the rice vinegar to a saucepan and bring to the boil. Slice the renkon, add it to the saucepan with the food colouring, remove from the heat and leave for at least 30 minutes. Drain and dry on kitchen paper. **THREE** Mix the sushi rice with the sesame seeds. Line an eggcup with a piece of clingfilm, 12 cm (5 inches) square. Place a slice of fish, a slice of renkon and a small dab of wasabi (if used) into the cup. Top with about 4 tablespoons sushi rice and twist the top of the clingfilm tightly. Pull out the moulded sushi in the clingfilm and shape it into a ball with your hands. Peel away the clingfilm and set the ball aside. Repeat this to make 6 balls. Make another 6 balls, using chives instead of renkon. **FOUR** Arrange the balls on a large plate or tray. Serve with the shoyu in an individual bowl to dip. Add more wasabi to the shoyu if a spicier taste is preferred.

Makes 12 balls; serves 3–6

NUTRIENT ANALYSIS PER SERVING 1464 kJ – 346 cal – 12 g protein – 70 g carbohydrate – 7 g sugars – 4 g fat – 0 g saturated fat – 2 g fibre – 463 mg sodium

HEALTHY TIP All fish is a good source of selenium, a trace mineral essential for preserving the body's natural anti-oxidant status.

White sashimi salad

Shiromi no sashimi salada When it is served at table, piping hot oil, drizzled over the raw fish, cooks it slightly. The crisp vegetables and crunchy nuts contrast with the texture of the fish.

INGREDIENTS *200 g (7 oz) carrots* ‖ *200 g (7 oz) leeks, trimmed* ‖ *200 g (7 oz) celery* ‖ *450 g (14½ oz) fresh white fish, such as flounder, sole, bream or snapper, filleted and skinned* ‖ *4 shiso leaves, cut lengthways into thin strips* ‖ *½ tablespoon vegetable oil* ‖ *150 g (5 oz) cashew nuts* ‖ *3 tablespoons roasted sesame oil* ‖ *1 garlic clove, crushed*

DRESSING *2 tablespoons shoyu* ‖ *2 tablespoons sake* ‖ *2 teaspoons lemon juice*

ONE Make the dressing by mixing together all the ingredients. Keep it in the refrigerator until it is required. **TWO** Cut the carrots, leeks and celery into julienne strips and soak thm in ice-cold water. **THREE** Remove all visible bones from the fish and cut the flesh across the grain into strips 1 cm (½ inch) thick. Mix together the fish and shiso leaves and keep in the refrigerator until required. **FOUR** Heat the oil in a small, nonstick fry pan and roast the cashew nuts until they are golden. Drain the nuts on kitchen paper and chop them roughly. Drain the vegetables and dry them well on kitchen paper. Put the fish in the middle of a large serving plate. Arrange the vegetables and nuts in 5 mounds around the fish. **FIVE** Just before serving, heat the sesame oil in a small, nonstick frying pan and cook the garlic. When the garlic turns golden, pour the hot oil over the fish, discarding the garlic. Mix everything at the table immediately and serve the dressing separately.

Serves 4 as a starter

NUTRIENT ANALYSIS PER SERVING 1830 kJ – 439 cal – 28 g protein – 13 g carbohydrate – 7 g sugars – 30 g fat – 5 g saturated fat – 4 g fibre – 696 mg sodium

HEALTHY TIP Carrots are an excellent source of beta-carotene, an important anti-oxidant that helps protect against some cancers.

Sushi with cooked fish topping *Mukashi nigiri* When hand-moulded nigiri sushi was originally made almost all the toppings were cooked.

INGREDIENTS *8 raw prawns, heads removed* ‖ *1 fresh fillet mackerel, bones removed* ‖ *2 tablespoons salt, plus extra for cooking* ‖ *2 tablespoons rice vinegar* ‖ *600 g (1¼ lb) cooked sushi rice (see page 17)* ‖ *1 cooked octopus tentacle, cut into 5 mm (¼ inch) slices* ‖ *1 fillet, about 100 g (3½ oz), cooked unagi eel or smoked eel* ‖ *2 teaspoons vegetable oil* ‖ *¼ sheet of nori, cut into 1 cm (½ inch) strips* ‖ *gari (see page 18), to garnish*

ATSUYAKI TAMAGO *150 ml (¼ pint) warm Dashi Stock (see page 18)* ‖ *½ teaspoon shoyu* ‖ *1 teaspoon mirin* ‖ *1 teaspoon sake* ‖ *2 teaspoons caster sugar* ‖ *¼ teaspoon salt* ‖ *6 eggs, beaten* ‖ *vegetable oil, for greasing*

ONE Mix together the stock, seasonings and eggs. Heat a square omelette pan and pour in a little oil. Remove from the heat and cool slightly. Return the pan to a medium heat and pour in one-third of the egg mixture. When it starts to bubble and set, lift the egg and roll it towards the end of the pan. Wipe the space with oiled paper and pour in another one-third of the egg mixture. Repeat with the remaining mixture. Remove from the heat and leave to stand for 2 minutes, then cut it into 8 pieces. **TWO** Skewer each prawn lengthways and boil in salted water until they turn red. Drain and remove the skewers and shells, but leave on the tails. Cut open from the belly side to lay prawns flat. **THREE** Thickly salt the mackerel fillet and leave for 20 minutes. Wash off the salt, then marinate in vinegar for 20 minutes. Wipe off the vinegar and peel off the top layer of skin. Cut the flesh across the grain into 8 slices, each 5 mm (¼ inch) thick, and set aside. **FOUR** Wet your fingers in *tezu (see page 46)* and scoop about 1½ tablespoons rice into your left palm. Shape it into a 3–4 cm (1¼–1½ inches) long brick. Make 32 sushi rice blocks, topping each block with a prawn or a piece of octopus, mackerel or eel. **FIVE** Make a slit in the centre of each piece of the omelette and fill with 1 teaspoon rice. Roll octopus sushi and tie each with a ribbon of nori. Garnish with gari.

Makes 32 pieces; serves 4

NUTRIENT ANALYSIS PER SERVING 1879 kJ – 448 cal – 27 g protein – 48 g carbohydrate – 7 g sugars – 17 g fat – 4 g saturated fat – 1 g fibre – 1397 mg sodium

HEALTHY TIP The combination of rice, fish and eggs makes this a very nutritious dish.

Easy sushi canapés *Kanappe zushi* Make this dish just before you serve it. Do not keep it in the refrigerator because sushi rice disintegrates and becomes unappetizing when it is chilled.

INGREDIENTS *4 sheets of nori* ‖ *600 g (1¼ lb) freshly cooked sushi rice (see page 18)* ‖ *200 g (7 oz) gari (see page 18), to serve*

TOPPING A *1 tablespoon mayonnaise* ‖ *1 teaspoon wasabi* ‖ *½ teaspoon shoyu* ‖ *½ medium avocado, peeled, stoned and sliced*

TOPPING B *1 egg, beaten* ‖ *¼ teaspoon salt* ‖ *½ teaspoon vegetable oil* ‖ *20 g (¾ oz) lump fish roe*

TOPPING C *10 amaebi sweet uncooked prawns* ‖ *½ teaspoon salt* ‖ *1 shiso leaf, chopped*

TOPPING D *1 slice smoked salmon, cut into 10 strips, each 2.5 cm (1 inch) wide* ‖ *2 tablespoons crème fraîche* ‖ *5 chives, cut in half*

ONE Mix together the ingredients for Topping A and set aside. Make a thick sushi roll. Place a rolling mat with the bamboo laid horizontally towards you. Lay a sheet of nori, shiny side down, on it. Spread one-quarter of the rice on the nori, leaving 1 cm (½ inch) space at the top. Roll up from the bottom edge, fold the rolled sushi with both hands and squeeze it gently to mould. **TWO** Spread another quarter of the rice on a piece of nori. Place the first roll at the bottom edge and roll. Repeat steps 1 and 2 to make a second roll. **THREE** Use a sharp knife to cut each roll into slices 1 cm (½ inch) wide. Wipe the knife with a damp cloth after every cut. **FOUR** Make Topping B – make soft scrambled egg and decorate with the fish roe. **FIVE** Make Topping C by peeling the prawns, leaving on the tails, and sprinkling them with the salt and shiso leaf. **SIX** Make Topping D by rolling up the strips of salmon around 2 pieces of chive and adding a little crème fraîche. **SEVEN** Spoon different toppings on to each of the canapé bases and serve with gari.

Makes 40 canapés

NUTRIENT ANALYSIS PER SERVING 130 kJ – 30 cal – 1 g protein – 5 g carbohydrate – 1 g sugars – 1 g fat – 0 g saturated fat – 0 g fibre – 100 mg sodium

HEALTHY TIP Seaweed is a good source of iodine, essential for the production of thyroid hormones.

Sprouted brown rice sushi in tofu pouches *Genmai*

inari You can find sprouted and dried brown rice (hatsuga genmai) in Japanese shops. It tastes sweeter and cooks faster than unsprouted brown rice. To make this at home, follow the method for bean sprouts *(see page 12)*. It takes 2–4 days to sprout and should be cooked before the roots reach 2 mm (¹⁄₁₆ inch) long. Cook in the same way as unsprouted brown rice.

INGREDIENTS *200 g (7 oz) brown rice, slightly sprouted* ‖ *50 g (2 oz) pinhead oats, rinsed* ‖ *50 g (2 oz) millet* ‖ *2½ tablespoons rice vinegar* ‖ *3½ tablespoons caster sugar* ‖ *½ teaspoon salt* ‖ *75 g (3 oz) pine nuts, roasted* ‖ *15 g (½ oz) roasted black sesame seeds* ‖ *10 abura age, rinsed in hot water and drained* ‖ *6 tablespoons shoyu* ‖ *2 tablespoons mirin* ‖ *2 tablespoons sake* ‖ *100 g (3½ oz) gari (see page 18),* **to serve**

ONE Cook the mixed grains in 650 ml (23 fl oz) water *(see page 17)*. **TWO** Transfer the cooked rice to a large bowl. Mix together the rice vinegar, 1½ tablespoons sugar and the salt and add to the rice. Stir in the pine nuts, sprinkle over the sesame seeds and cover the bowl with a wet cloth. **THREE** Meanwhile, squeeze the water from the abura age and cut each in half. Gently open the cut edge to make a pouch but take care that you do not break the skin. Repeat to make 20 pouches. **FOUR** Put 400 ml (14 fl oz) water in a saucepan and add the shoyu, mirin, sake and 2 tablespoons sugar. Cook the abura age in the seasoned water over a low heat until the liquid has reduced to about one-quarter. Drain into a sieve and leave to cool. **FIVE** Half-fill a pouch with cooled rice, making a triangle by folding the opening diagonally into each pouch before filling it with sushi rice. Serve at room temperature with gari.

Makes 20; serves 4

NUTRIENT ANALYSIS PER SERVING 3090 kJ – 737 cal – 29 g protein – 86 g carbohydrate – 24 g sugars – 31 g fat – 2 g saturated fat – 3 g fibre – 1650 mg sodium

HEALTHY TIP Sprouted brown rice has many unusual nutritional attributes, including GABA (gamma-antibiotic acid), which is effective in lowering blood pressure, inositl, which is calming, and fitchen acid, which is believed to have anti-cancer properties.

Vegetarian chirashi sushi

Shojin chirashi Chirashi is a domestic-style sushi. It is rather like a rice salad, and numerous variations are made for party food or for quick lunches. This colourful chirashi would be an excellent centrepiece for a party.

INGREDIENTS *600 g (1¼ lb) freshly cooked sushi rice (see page 18)* ‖ *1 tablespoon roasted white sesame seeds* ‖ *1 tablespoon roasted black sesame seeds* ‖ *500 g (1 lb) shelled broad beans* ‖ *400 ml (14 fl oz) Dashi Stock (see page 19)* ‖ *2 tablespoons mirin* ‖ *1⅓ teaspoons salt* ‖ *1 large carrot, peeled and cut into juliennes* ‖ *2 teaspoons vegetable oil* ‖ *1 egg, beaten*

ONE While the rice is still warm mix it with the with sesame seeds. **TWO** Cook the broad beans in lightly salted water, drain and remove the skins. **THREE** Put the stock in a heavy-based saucepan. Bring it to the boil and add the mirin and 1 teaspoon salt, then the carrot. Cook for 3 minutes, then remove from the heat and leave to cool. **FOUR** Heat the oil in a 23–25 cm (9–10 inch) nonstick frying pan and wipe away any excess oil with kitchen paper. Reduce the heat to low. Mix the egg with the remaining salt and use a spoon to draw some lines with one-quarter of the egg in the frying pan to make a round lattice. Remove from the heat until dry, then carefully lift out the egg with a palette knife. Repeat to make 4 lattices and set aside. **FIVE** Drain the carrot and squeeze out any moisture. Pile rice on 4 plates. Spread broad beans and carrot over the rice and cover the top with the egg. Serve at room temperature with a clear soup.

Serves 4

NUTRIENT ANALYSIS PER SERVING 1447 kJ – 344 cal – 13 g protein – 56 g carbohydrate – 8 g sugars – 8 g fat – 1 g saturated fat – 2 g fibre – 835 mg sodium

HEALTHY TIP Sesame seeds are highly nutritious, with a high calcium content. Combining seeds with grains enhances the protein content of each constituent.

Fish and seafood

Seared salmon sashimi salad
Sake no tataki salada The soft salmon flesh and roe will melt in your mouth. If you cannot find awakuchi or usukuchi shoyu (pale soy sauce) use ordinary shoyu instead. Salted salmon roe is sold in jars and is available in some supermarkets and in Japanese and oriental stores.

INGREDIENTS *olive oil, for frying* ‖ *400 g (13 oz) salmon fillet for sashimi or sushi, lightly salted and at room temperature* ‖ *½ yellow pepper, deseeded and cut into 5 mm (¼ inch) squares* ‖ *4 mini cucumbers, finely sliced* ‖ *handful of mizuna or rocket leaves* ‖ *4 tablespoons ikura (salted salmon roe), to garnish*

DRESSING *rind and juice of 1 lemon* ‖ *100 ml (3½ fl oz) extra virgin olive oil* ‖ *1 teaspoon awakuchi or usukuchi shoyu (pale soy sauce)* ‖ *1 teaspoon wholegrain mustard*

ONE Heat a little olive oil in a nonstick frying pan and wipe away any excess with kitchen paper. Sear the salmon for 45 seconds on each side. Plunge the fish into a bowl of ice-cold water to prevent further cooking, then pat it dry with a tea towel. **TWO** Make the dressing by mixing together all the ingredients. Add the yellow pepper and set aside. **THREE** Slice the salmon fillet thinly across the grain. Arrange the cucumber slices in horizontal rows on 4 plates. **FOUR** Place one-quarter of the mizuna leaves in the centre of each and pour over a little dressing. Arrange slices of salmon over the mizuna. Garnish with salmon roe and drizzle the remaining dressing over the plate. Serve immediately.

Serves 4

NUTRIENT ANALYSIS PER SERVING 1687 kJ – 407 cal – 23 g protein – 1 g carbohydrate – 1 g sugars – 34 g fat – 5 g saturated fat – 1 g fibre – 660 mg sodium

HEALTHY TIP Salmon is a fatty fish and thus a good source of omega-3 fatty acids, which may help to protect against blood clotting and some cancers.

Grilled seafood skewers

Kaisen kushi-yaki Umeboshi (pickled plum) is very sour and salty. It is often eaten in small quantities with a bowl of plain rice, but the combination of flavours takes some getting used to. When it is used in a marinade or dressing, the sourness diminishes and adds a more complex flavour to other ingredients, including seafood.

INGREDIENTS *1 large squid tube, about 150 g (5 oz), skinned and tentacles and guts removed, or 150 g (5 oz) baby squid* ‖ *4 large uncooked prawns* ‖ *4 large, live clams in their shells* ‖ *2 tentacles boiled octopus, cut into bite-sized pieces* ‖ *½ cucumber, cut into sticks* ‖ *½ red pepper, deseeded and cut into sticks* ‖ *¼ firm white cabbage, cut into 5 cm (2 inch) ribbons*

PLUM MARINADE *4–6 umeboshi (pickled plums), stoned and puréed* ‖ *4 tablespoons shoyu* ‖ *3 tablespoons mirin* ‖ *2 tablespoons sake*

ONE Soak 20 bamboo skewers in water overnight. Cut open the squid tube to make it flat and use a sharp knife to score the skin with crisscross cuts. Cut it crossways into strips 2.5 cm (1 inch) wide. Shell the prawns, leaving on the heads and tails. **TWO** Mix together all the ingredients for the marinade and marinate the squid, prawns and octopus pieces for 20 minutes in the refrigerator. **THREE** Drain the seafood (reserve the marinade) and thread the pieces on to bamboo skewers. Cook on a preheated griddle or under a preheated hot grill for a few minutes each side, brushing with the marinade from time to time. Cook the clams on a griddle until the shells open. Pour 1 teaspoon of the reserved marinade into each clam shell and remove from the heat. (Discard any clams that have not opened.) **FOUR** Put any remaining marinade in a saucepan and bring it to the boil. Remove from the heat and leave to cool, then pour it into a small dish to serve as a dipping sauce. Arrange the skewers on a plate and serve with the vegetables.

Serves 4

NUTRIENT ANALYSIS PER SERVING 535 kJ – 128 cal – 17 g protein – 7 g carbohydrate – 5 g sugars – 1 g fat – 0 g saturated fat – 2 g fibre – 1400 mg sodium

HEALTHY TIP Seafood is a good source of selenium and a natural anti-oxidant.

Swordfish teriyaki with fruit sauce *Kajiki no teriyaki* This

special teriyaki sauce with marmalade and orange goes well with the delicate flavour of swordfish. Avoid overcooking so that the fish does not become dry and leathery.

INGREDIENTS *4 swordfish steaks, about 500 g (1 lb) in total* ‖ *1 tablespoon vegetable oil, plus extra for greasing* ‖ *125 g (4 oz) shimeji mushrooms, separated* ‖ *½ onion, thinly sliced vertically* ‖ *1 small green pepper, deseeded and cut into rings* ‖ *⅓ orange, peeled and segmented* ‖ *rice, to serve*

FRUIT SAUCE *4 tablespoons shoyu* ‖ *3 tablespoons low-sugar orange marmalade* ‖ *2 tablespoons mirin*

ONE Make the fruit sauce by mixing together the ingredients. Put the fish in a non-metallic dish, pour over the sauce and leave to marinate for 1–3 hours. **TWO** Remove the fish from the marinade (reserve the marinade) and wipe the fish with kitchen paper. Lightly oil a baking sheet and cook the fish in a preheated oven, 220°C (425°F), Gas Mark 7, for 9 minutes. Turn the fish over and brush with the marinade. Reduce the oven temperature to 180°C (350°F), Gas Mark 4, and cook for a further 5 minutes. **THREE** Heat the oil in a frying pan and stir-fry the mushrooms, onion, green pepper and orange segments. Pour over the remaining marinade and stir until the pepper is cooked but still crunchy. **FOUR** Transfer the fish to 4 plates with the warm vegetables and serve with a bowl of rice.

Serves 4

NUTRIENT ANALYSIS PER SERVING 926 kJ – 220 cal – 25 g protein – 14 g carbohydrate – 2 g sugars – 8 g fat – 1 g saturated fat – 1 g fibre – 1060 mg sodium

HEALTHY TIP Green peppers and oranges are high in the anti-oxidant beta-carotene, which is believed to help protect against blood clotting and some forms of cancer.

Kyoto-style mackerel and hakusai leaves *Hakusai to saba no nimono* The combination of oily mackerel and gently cooked hakusai (Chinese cabbage) makes a comforting everyday dish. You can use canned mackerel if fresh fish is not available.

INGREDIENTS *2 whole mackerel, cleaned and filleted* ‖ *½ hakusai (Chinese cabbage), core removed and cut into 5 cm (2 inch) pieces* ‖ *3 tablespoons shoyu* ‖ *3 tablespoons sake* ‖ *5 cm (2 inches) fresh root ginger, peeled and thinly sliced* ‖ *rind of ½ lemon, to garnish* ‖ *short grain rice, to serve*

ONE Cut each mackerel fillet crossways into 3–4 slices. **TWO** Put the pieces of cabbage in a heavy-based saucepan and arrange the mackerel on top. Gently pour in 200 ml (7 fl oz) water, the shoyu and sake and scatter over the ginger slices. **THREE** Cover the pan and cook over a moderate heat for 5 minutes. Reduce the heat to low and simmer for a further 15 minutes or until the cabbage is quite soft. **FOUR** Carefully transfer the cabbage and mackerel to a large bowl and pour in the remaining liquid. Sprinkle over the lemon rind and serve warm with a bowl of rice.

Serves 4

NUTRIENT ANALYSIS PER SERVING 1286 kJ – 310 cal – 26 g protein – 2 g carbohydrate – 1 g sugars – 21 g fat – 4 g saturated fat – 0 g fibre – 813 mg sodium

HEALTHY TIP Mackerel is a particularly good source of omega-3 fatty acids, which may have a role in protecting against blood clotting and some cancers. It is also a good source of vitamin D, essential for bone growth and maintenance.

Grilled prawns in spring rolls

Ebi no koromo makiyaki These prawns, wrapped in a crispy coating, can be eaten with the fingers, and they make a good party food. The whole prawn can be eaten because the head and tail become crisp. If you cannot find spring roll wrappers, use filo pastry instead.

INGREDIENTS *20 uncooked prawns* ‖ *2 tablespoons wasabi* ‖ *2 spring onions, cut into thin strips* ‖ *½ sheet of nori, cut into strips* ‖ *5 spring roll wrappers, each cut into 4 squares* ‖ *1 tablespoon plain flour* ‖ *3 tablespoons vegetable oil, plus extra for greasing* ‖ *1 teaspoon salt*

ONE Shell the prawns, leaving on the heads and tails. Trim the whiskers and cut off the tips of the tails. **TWO** Insert a skewer into each prawn to stop it curling. Smear wasabi over each prawn and put some spring onion and nori strips on it. Roll the prawn in a piece of spring roll wrapper. Mix the flour with 2 teaspoons water and use the mixture to seal the ends of the rolls. **THREE** Place the prawn rolls on a lightly oiled baking sheet and brush them with oil. Cook on a griddle or under a preheated grill for 6–7 minutes, turning once, until the spring roll wrappers are golden and crispy. Sprinkle with salt and serve hot.

Makes 20; serves 4

NUTRIENT ANALYSIS PER SERVING 805 kJ – 194 cal – 9 g protein – 14 g carbohydrate – 1 g sugars – 11 g fat – 1 g saturated fat – 1 g fibre – 640 mg sodium

HEALTHY TIP Prawns do contain cholesterol, but possibly in a form which is not particularly harmful. To protect against high blood cholesterol levels it is more important to limit total fat intake than to restrict dietary cholesterol.

Squid with yakumi sauce

Ika no yakumi gake If you have had any unfortunate encounters with rubbery squid dishes that have been cooked inappropriately, this recipe might redeem the experience.

INGREDIENTS *450 g (14½ oz) squid tubes, skinned and tentacles and guts removed* ‖ *1 shiso leaf, cut into strips, to garnish*

YAKUMI SAUCE *3 spring onions, chopped* ‖ *200 g (7 oz) cucumber, chopped* ‖ *40 g (1½ oz) za cai (Sichuan pickled vegetables), finely chopped* ‖ *3 shiso leaves, finely chopped* ‖ *4 tablespoons shoyu* ‖ *4 tablespoons water* ‖ *4 tablespoons rice vinegar* ‖ *2 tablespoons roasted sesame oil* ‖ *2 teaspoons honey*

ONE Make the sauce by mixing together all the ingredients. Set it aside. **TWO** Meanwhile, cut open the squid tube lengthways to make it flat. Use a sharp knife to score the skin with crisscross cuts. Cut the flesh into 2 x 5 cm (¾ x 2 inches) strips. **THREE** Boil the squid in water for 2–3 minutes or until it is milky white and the strips curl up. Drain well. **FOUR** Place the warm squid on a large plate and pour the sauce over it. Garnish with the strips of shiso and serve immediately.

Serves 4

NUTRIENT ANALYSIS PER SERVING 690 kJ – 165 cal – 20 g protein – 6 g carbohydrate – 4 g sugars – 7 g fat – 1 g saturated fat – 1 g fibre – 1460 mg sodium

HEALTHY TIP Cucumber is high in water, with a low calorie content. It is thought to have a diuretic effect and may help in reducing blood pressure.

Miso grilled scorpion fish

Kasagoi misoyaki Scorpion fish (*kasago*) is popular in many European countries, including Italy, France and Greece, as well as in Southeast Asia. The liver is regarded as a delicacy, although the spiny dorsal and pectoral fins are mildly poisonous. Use red bream or snapper if you cannot find scorpion fish.

INGREDIENTS *4 whole scorpion fish* ‖ *1 spring onion* ‖ *1 tablespoon miso* ‖ *handful of rocket leaves* ‖ *salt* ‖ *280 g (9½ oz) shelled broad beans, boiled in salted water, to serve*

NON-OIL MAYONNAISE *2 egg yolks, beaten* ‖ *2 teaspoons plain flour* ‖ *2 teaspoons salt* ‖ *1½ tablespoons caster sugar* ‖ *4 tablespoons rice vinegar* ‖ *2 tablespoons sake* ‖ *2 teaspoons mustard powder*

ONE Make the mayonnaise. Whisk together the egg yolks, flour, salt and sugar in a bowl, then add the vinegar and sake. Strain the mixture into a saucepan and simmer over a low heat until the sauce thickens. Stir in the mustard powder and leave to cool. The mayonnaise will keep for up to 3 days in the refrigerator. **TWO** Cut the dorsal fins from the scorpion fish and trim off the tips of the pectoral fins. Insert a sharp knife from the top of the fish. Cut along the bones and open up the upper half of the fish's body. Leave the guts inside. Sprinkle with salt. **THREE** Leaving the white part whole, finely chop the green part of the spring onion. Mix the mayonnaise with the miso and chopped spring onion. Arrange the fish on a lightly oiled baking sheet so that the cuts in the back are uppermost and stuff the cavities with the mayonnaise mixture. Leave for 15 minutes. **FOUR** Arrange rocket leaves and the white part of the spring onion over the fish and cook under a preheated hot grill for 5 minutes. Cover the fish with a piece of foil and cook for a further 5–7 minutes. **FIVE** Meanwhile, skin the broad beans by making a small cut in the top of the bean and pop the insides into a bowl. Sprinkle with a little salt. Serve the fish warm with the broad beans.

Serves 4

NUTRIENT ANALYSIS PER SERVING 1028 kJ – 244 cal – 27 g protein – 17 g carbohydrate – 9 g sugars – 8 g fat – 1 g saturated fat – 3 g fibre – 1414 mg sodium

HEALTHY TIP Look for a lower salt brand of miso to reduce the high salt content of this dish.

Steamed clams in sake

Asari saka maushi Fresh clams are steamed with just a little sake, the simple cooking bringing out all the rich fragrance of the sea from the shellfish. This dish goes well with rice dishes, such as Redbush Tea Pilaf with Walnuts *(see page 134)*.

INGREDIENTS *1 kg (2 lb) fresh live clams* ‖ *6 tablespoons sake* ‖ *1 bunch of chives, finely chopped* ‖ *shoyu, to taste* ‖ *salt*

ONE Soak the clams in cold, salted water for at least 2 hours to remove any grit. Drain and wash them under running water, discarding any clams that are open or that have broken shells. **TWO** Put the clams in a deep, heavy-based saucepan with the sake. Cover and cook over a moderate heat until all the shells have opened. Discard any that are closed. **THREE** Add the chives and check the taste, adding a little shoyu if wished, then remove from the heat. Serve hot with the cooking liquid from the saucepan.

Serves 4

NUTRIENT ANALYSIS PER SERVING 289 kJ – 70 cal – 8 g protein – 2 g carbohydrate -– 0 g sugars – 1 g fat – 0 g saturated fat – 0 g fibre – 36 mg sodium

HEALTHY TIP Clams are a good source of the trace minerals iodine and selenium. Iodine is essential for thyroid hormone production.

Prawn, scallop and broccoli stir-fry *Ebi to hoate no burokkori itame* The silky sauce in this quick and easy Chinese-style recipe compliments the seafood and vegetables. Tobiko flying fish roe) resembles caviar but is less expensive and has a milder flavour.

INGREDIENTS *1 large broccoli, stem removed and separated into florets* ‖ *2 tablespoons roasted sesame oil* ‖ *2.5 cm (1 inch) fresh root ginger, peeled and finely sliced* ‖ *500 g (1 lb) cooked peeled prawns* ‖ *4 scallops, cut into 3–4 slices* ‖ *2 tablespoons sake* ‖ *400 ml (14 fl oz) hot Dashi Stock (see page 19)* ‖ *1½ teaspoons salt* ‖ *2 teaspoons shoyu* ‖ *2 teaspoons arrowroot* ‖ *4 tablespoons tobiko (flying fish roe) or lump fish roe* ‖ *rice, to serve*

ONE Blanch the broccoli in lightly salted water for 3 minutes. Drain and keep warm. **TWO** Heat the oil in a large, nonstick frying pan and stir-fry the ginger. Add the prawns and scallops and cook over a high heat for a further 2 minutes. Pour in the sake and hot stock. Add the salt and shoyu. **THREE** Mix the arrowroot with 2 teaspoons water and stir into the mixture. When the liquid has thickened add the broccoli. Remove from the heat. **FOUR** Stir in the fish roe and serve immediately with a bowl of rice.

Serves 4

NUTRIENT ANALYSIS PER SERVING 1180 kJ – 280 cal – 42 g protein – 6 g carbohydrate – 2 g sugars – 9 g fat – 2 g saturated fat – 1 g fibre – 2957 mg sodium

HEALTHY TIP Broccoli is a good source of folate, essential for cell formation and thus important in early pregnancy. Folate is destroyed by heat, so broccoli should be cooked as lightly as possible.

Marinated fried whitebait

Nanban duke The practice of frying fish in oil and then quickly marinating it in a vinaigrette dressing is believed to have been brought to Japan from southern Europe, and it is now widely used for cooking small fish such as whitebait.

INGREDIENTS *4 tablespoons plain flour* ‖ *1½ teaspoons salt* ‖ *450 g (14½ oz) whitebait* ‖ *vegetable oil, for deep-frying* ‖ *2 garlic cloves, peeled and thinly sliced* ‖ *1 onion, cut into juliennes* ‖ *1 large carrot, cut into juliennes* ‖ *1 green pepper, deseeded and cut into juliennes* ‖ *2–3 lettuce leaves, torn into pieces, to serve*

MARINADE *400 ml (14 fl oz) Dashi Stock (see page 19)* ‖ *2 tablespoons sake* ‖ *4 tablespoons honey* ‖ *180 ml (6¼ fl oz) rice vinegar* ‖ *2 tablespoons shoyu* ‖ *1 dried red chilli, deseeded and finely chopped* ‖ *1 teaspoon salt*

ONE Make the marinade. Mix together all the ingredients in a large saucepan and bring to the boil, remove from heat and set aside. **TWO** Mix the flour with the salt and use the mixture to coat the fish. Heat oil to a depth of 2.5 cm (1 inch) to 180°C (350°F) in a deep frying pan. Fry the garlic slices until they are crisp, remove them from the pan and drain on kitchen paper. Deep-fry the fish, in 2 batches, for 3–4 minutes or until they are golden. **THREE** Drain the fish on kitchen paper and then plunge them into the marinade while it is still hot. Add the garlic slices and vegetables and leave to marinate for at least 30 minutes. **FOUR** Arrange the pieces of lettuce on 4 plates. Remove the fish and vegetables from the marinade with a fork or chopsticks and arrange them on top of the lettuce. (Any remaining marinade should be discarded.) Serve while the fish is still warm. Alternatively, the dish will keep for up to 3 days in the refrigerator and can be eaten cold.

Serves 4

NUTRIENT ANALYSIS PER SERVING 2655 kJ – 637 cal – 21 g protein – 44 g carbohydrate – 23 g sugars – 42 g fat – 4 g saturated fat – 2 g fibre – 1890 mg sodium

HEALTHY TIP When fried fish is quickly marinated in vinaigrette the oil is washed away. Deep-frying makes the entire fish edible and is therefore an efficient way to obtain omega-3 oil and high-quality calcium from the bones.

Monkfish with seaweed and pepper sauce *Ankou no wakame sosu*

This is a good recipe to try if you have not eaten seaweed before because it is not easy to identify the green flecks in the white sauce as seaweed and not some other green leaf. Wakame is usually sold trimmed, chopped and dried, but if you are using untrimmed wakame, soak it in warm water then cut off the hard stalk that runs up the centre of the leaf.

INGREDIENTS *700 g (1 lb 7 oz) monkfish fillet, skinned and cut into 2.5 cm (1 inch) pieces* ‖ *1 teaspoon salt* ‖ *2 tablespoons plain flour* ‖ *2 tablespoons olive oil* ‖ *5 g (¼ oz) dried cut wakame, soaked in warm water for 10 minutes* ‖ *160 g (5½ oz) spinach leaves, washed* ‖ *400 ml (14 fl oz) unsweetened soya milk* ‖ *1 tablespoon plain flour* ‖ *1 tablespoon white or yellow miso* ‖ *2 tablespoons grated Parmesan cheese* ‖ *1 tablespoon cracked green peppercorns* ‖ *75 g (3 oz) watercress, to garnish*

ONE Sprinkle the fish with salt and coat it with plain flour. **TWO** Heat the oil in a nonstick frying pan and cook the fish for 5–7 minutes over a moderate heat, turning the pieces a few times until they are evenly cooked. Remove from the pan and keep warm. **THREE** Meanwhile, blanch the wakame and spinach in boiling salted water for 2 minutes. Drain and soak in cold water to prevent further cooking. Squeeze out the water and chop finely. **FOUR** Whisk together the milk and flour and heat gently until the mixture thickens. Add the miso little by little. Remove from the heat and stir in the cheese, peppercorns, wakame and spinach. **FIVE** Transfer the fish to 4 plates and spoon over the sauce. Garnish with watercress and serve immediately.

Serves 4

NUTRIENT ANALYSIS PER SERVING 1235 kJ – 293 cal – 36 g protein – 14 g carbohydrate – 2 g sugars – 11 g fat – 2 g saturated fat – 3 g fibre – 847 mg sodium

HEALTHY TIP When buying soya milk check that it is high in calcium and, if possible, enriched with fat-soluble vitamins A and D.

Steamed salmon parcels with vegetables *Sake no hosho mushi*

The salmon is steamed in its own juices and sake, and a rich aroma arises when the paper parcels are opened at the table. Nira chives or Chinese chives are available from oriental stores and in some large supermarkets.

INGREDIENTS *1 teaspoon salt* ‖ *4 salmon fillets, about 600 g (1¼ lb) in total, skinned* ‖ *15 g (½ oz) butter, at room temperature* ‖ *125 g (4 oz) shimeji mushrooms, trimmed* ‖ *½ onion, thinly sliced* ‖ *80 g (3¼ oz) nira chives or 4 spring onions, cut into 5 cm (2 inch) pieces* ‖ *2 tablespoons sake* ‖ *rice, to serve*

ONE Cut 4 squares of greaseproof paper or baking parchment, each 30 x 30 cm (12 x 12 inches). Fold each square in half diagonally, open it out and grease one side with butter. **TWO** Sprinkle salt over the salmon and place a fillet in the centre of the greased paper along the folded line. Arrange a quarter of the mushrooms, onion and chives on each piece of salmon. Sprinkle over ½ tablespoon sake and a pinch of salt. **THREE** Fold opposite points of the triangle together and roll and fold the sides to make a parcel. Twist both ends together. Repeat with the remaining ingredients to make 4 parcels. **FOUR** Pour water into a baking tin to a depth of 1 cm (½ inch). Place the parcels in the water and cook in a preheated oven, 180°C (350°F), Gas Mark 4, for 15 minutes or until the parcels are puffed up. **FIVE** Serve the parcels on 4 plates, with rice, and ask your guests to open them at the table.

Serves 4

NUTRIENT ANALYSIS PER SERVING 1334 kJ – 320 cal – 29 g protein – 2 g carbohydrate – 1 g sugars – 21 g fat – 5 g saturated fat – 0 g fibre – 687 mg sodium

HEALTHY TIP Salmon is a high-fat fish and therefore high in calories. The type of fat in salmon is mostly polyunsaturated, with an important content of omega-3 fatty acids.

Meat and poultry

Marinated and steamed pork fillet *Buta no sakamushi*

The sake gives the meat a rich flavour, while steaming the pork helps to reduce the fat content of the dish.

INGREDIENTS *300 g (10 oz) pork fillet (tenderloin)* ‖ *2 tablespoons sake or dry sherry* ‖ *2 teaspoons coarse sea salt* ‖ *2.5 cm (1 inch) fresh root ginger, peeled, finely sliced lengthways and soaked in ice-cold water* ‖ *2 spring onions (white part only), cut in half, finely sliced lengthways and soaked in ice-cold water* ‖ *1 small lettuce, such as red leaf or cos (romaine), separated and washed*

SAUCE *2 tablespoons shoyu* ‖ *2 tablespoons rice vinegar* ‖ *1½ tablespoons roasted sesame oil* ‖ *2 teaspoons roasted white sesame seeds* ‖ *2 garlic cloves, grated or finely chopped* ‖ *2.5 cm (1 inch) fresh root ginger, peeled and grated or finely chopped* ‖ *1 dried red chilli, deseeded and chopped*

ONE Put the meat in a non-metallic, ovenproof dish and sprinkle over the sake. Rub the sake into the meat with your hands, cover the dish and leave for 3 hours or overnight in the refrigerator, turning occasionally. Take the dish out of the refrigerator a few hours before cooking. **TWO** Put the dish containing the meat in a steamer with a lid. Steam the meat over a simmering heat for 20 minutes or until it is cooked through but still slightly pink inside. Turn off the heat and sprinkle the salt over the pork. Leave the meat inside the steamer, uncovered, until it is cool. Reserve the liquid left in the dish. **THREE** Meanwhile, make the sauce by mixing together all the ingredients with 2 tablespoons of the cooking liquid. **FOUR** Cut the meat into slices 5 mm (¼ inch) thick. Drain the ginger and spring onion threads. **FIVE** Arrange the meat on a bed of lettuce leaves with the ginger and spring onion threads, spoon over the sauce and serve.

Serves 4

NUTRIENT ANALYSIS PER SERVING 865 kJ – 207 cal – 18 g protein – 2 g carbohydrate – 1 g sugars – 13 g fat – 3 g saturated fat – 0 g fibre – 1460 mg sodium

HEALTHY TIP Pork is higher in fat than red meat, but modern rearing methods have reduced the traditionally high fat level of pork. Buy lean pork and cut off all visible fat.

Japanese-style white meatloaf *Torihiki yaki* This light, low-calorie

meatloaf contains chicken, soya beans and ginger, all of which help to maintain good health.

INGREDIENTS *400 g (13 oz) boneless and skinless chicken breast, minced or finely chopped* ‖ *60 g (2¼ oz) dried soya beans* ‖ *2 teaspoons vegetable oil* ‖ *1 large onion, finely chopped* ‖ *3 tablespoons arrowroot or cornflour* ‖ *2.5 cm (1 inch) fresh root ginger, peeled, grated and squeezed* ‖ *¼ teaspoon salt* ‖ *16 French green beens* ‖ *12 hard-boiled quail eggs, shelled*

SAUCE *2 tablespoons sake* ‖ *2 tablespoons oyster sauce* ‖ *1 tablespoon honey* ‖ *1 tablespoon arrowroot*

ONE Wash and soak the dried beans in warm water overnight. Drain the beans and transfer them to a heavy-based saucepan. Cover with water to double their depth. Bring to the boil, then simmer until the beans are tender. Leave to cool. **TWO** Heat the oil in a nonstick frying pan and cook the onion until it is translucent. Allow the onion to cool slightly, then transfer it to a food processor with the chicken, soya beans, arrowroot, ginger juice, salt and 3 tablespoons water. Blend until smooth. **THREE** Line a 500 g (1 lb) terrine mould or cake tin with greaseproof paper. Pour one-third of the mixture into the mould. Arrange half the beans and eggs on the mixture and pour in a further third of the mixture. Arrange the remaining beans and eggs on top and cover with remaining mixture. Shake the tin gently to remove any air and cover the top with a foil. **FOUR** Cook the loaf in a preheated oven, 180°C (350°F), Gas Mark 4, for 20 minutes. Insert a skewer and if clear juice runs out, the meat is cooked. **FIVE** Make the sauce. Mix together the sake, oyster sauce and honey in a saucepan and heat gently. Mix the arrowroot with 1 tablespoon water and stir in slowly to thicken the sauce. Slice the meatloaf and serve warm with the sauce.

Serves 4

NUTRIENT ANALYSIS PER SERVING 1364 kJ – 324 cal – 32 g protein – 23 g carbohydrate – 9 g sugars – 11 g fat – 2 g saturated fat – 1 g fibre – 640 mg sodium

HEALTHY TIP Soya beans are high in protein and a good source of iron and zinc. Zinc is essential for the repair of body tissue.

Steamed chicken with a tangy vegetable sauce *Mushi dori no kurosu an kake*

The thick, chocolate-coloured sauce is made with Japanese black vinegar, and it makes the steamed chicken taste as if it has been fried in oil. This dish goes well with salads such as Hakusai, Cottage Cheese and Goji Berry Salad *(see page 112)*.

INGREDIENTS *4 chicken breasts (with skins)* ‖ *4 spring onions, cut into 5 cm (2 inch) lengths* ‖ *100 ml (3½ fl oz) sake* ‖ *½ teaspoon salt* ‖ *salad, to serve*

VEGETABLE SAUCE *1 tablespoon vegetable oil* ‖ *1 small carrot, finely chopped* ‖ *15 cm (6 inch) celery stalk, finely chopped* ‖ *¼ red pepper, deseeded and finely chopped* ‖ *¼ onion, finely chopped* ‖ *4 teaspoons kurosu (Japanese black vinegar) or balsamic vinegar* ‖ *4 teaspoons honey* ‖ *2 tablespoons shoyu*

ONE Put the chicken, spring onions, sake and salt in a plastic bag. Make sure the meat is coated with the marinade and leave in the refrigerator for 30 minutes. **TWO** Make the sauce. Heat the oil in a nonstick frying pan and cook the carrot, celery, red pepper and onion. Add the remaining ingredients, cover and simmer over a low heat for 6–7 minutes. **THREE** Transfer the chicken and marinade to an ovenproof bowl and cover with clingfilm. **FOUR** Cook the meat in a hot steamer for 12 minutes, then remove from the heat and leave for 10 minutes. Remove the skin from the chicken and cut the flesh into slices 8 mm (⅓ inch) thick. Keep them in a bowl with the cooking liquid. **FIVE** Arrange the chicken on 4 individual plates (discarding any remaining marinade) and spoon over the sauce. Serve warm with a salad.

Serves 4

NUTRIENT ANALYSIS PER SERVING 1600 kJ – 384 cal – 32 g protein – 10 g carbohydrate –9 g sugars – 22 g fat – 6 g saturated fat – 1 g fibre – 774 mg sodium

HEALTHY TIP Most of the fat in chicken is in the skin, so discarding the skin after cooking will reduce the fat content of the dish.

Rice-coated meatballs

Dattan fu mochigome mushi These delicious lamb meatballs, coated with steamed rice, gleam like small gemstones.

INGREDIENTS *100 g (3½ oz) mochigome (extra glutinous rice)* ‖ *300 g (10 oz) minced lean lamb* ‖ *½ onion, finely chopped* ‖ *1 teaspoon caster sugar* ‖ *1 teaspoon shoyu* ‖ *⅓ teaspoons dried ground sage* ‖ *1 teaspoon salt*

DIPPING SAUCE *50 ml (2 fl oz) white wine* ‖ *1 small onion, quartered* ‖ *1 apple, cored and quartered* ‖ *4 tablespoons lemon juice* ‖ *2.5 cm (1 inch) fresh root ginger, peeled and crushed* ‖ *2 garlic cloves, crushed* ‖ *3 tablespoons shoyu* ‖ *⅓ teaspoon ground cinnamon* ‖ *½ teaspoon salt*

TO SERVE *3–4 lettuce leaves* ‖ *English or Japanese yellow mustard*

ONE Wash the rice, soak it in water for 3 hours and then leave it to drain for 30 minutes. **TWO** Make the sauce. Put the wine in a saucepan, heat it and let it bubble for 3 minutes, then remove the pan from the heat. Add all the other ingredients, transfer to a food processor and blend to make a smooth paste. Set aside. **THREE** Use your hands to mix together the meat and onion in a bowl. Add the sugar, shoyu, sage and salt and roll the mixture into balls about 3 cm (1¼ inches) across. **FOUR** Spread the rice over a tray and roll the meatballs carefully over the rice until they are evenly coated. Do not force the grains into the meatballs or the rice will not cook properly. **FIVE** Line a preheated steamer with an old tea towel or several layers of kitchen paper. Place the meatballs in the steamer and cook over a high heat for 15 minutes or until the rice is cooked. Leave to cool slightly. **SIX** Dampen your fingers and lift the meatballs from the steamer. Arrange them on a bed of lettuce leaves and serve warm with dipping sauce and mustard.

Makes 16 meatballs; serves 4

NUTRIENT ANALYSIS PER SERVING 1055 kJ – 250 cal – 19 g protein – 25 g carbohydrate – 5 g sugars – 7 g fat – 3 g saturated fat – 1 g fibre – 1512 mg sodium

HEALTHY TIP Combining a starchy food such as rice with meat increases the value and availability of the protein in the food.

Duck and leek hotpot *Kamo nabe* This dish is supposed to be cooked at the dinner table, like cheese fondue. The liquid left in the pot after all the vegetables and meat have been eaten makes a superb soup by itself, or it can be eaten with cooked udon noodles to finish off the meal.

INGREDIENTS *1 teaspoon vegetable oil* ‖ *3 boneless duck breasts* ‖ *½ hakusai (Chinese cabbage), cut lengthways into 5 cm (2 inch) pieces* ‖ *1 leek, cut into 5 cm (2 inch) pieces* ‖ *about 125 g (4 oz) enoki mushrooms, trimmed* ‖ *1 tablespoon sake* ‖ *1.2 litres (2 pints) Dashi Stock (see page 19)* ‖ *250 g (8 oz) mizuna or rocket leaves* ‖ *sansho (Japanese pepper) and salt, to taste*

DIPPING SAUCE *4 tablespoons orange juice* ‖ *4 tablespoons shoyu* ‖ *1 teaspoon honey* ‖ *5 g (¼ oz) katsuo bushi (dried bonito flakes)* ‖ *piece of konbu (kelp), 5 cm (2 inches) square, cut into strips*

ONE Make the dipping sauce by mixing together all the ingredients in a bowl. Leave for at least an hour or overnight for the flavours to blend, then strain into a dish and set on the table. **TWO** Heat the oil in a nonstick frying pan and cook the duck over a moderate heat, turning frequently, for about 5 minutes. Leave the duck to cool slightly, then drain on kitchen paper. Cut the meat into slices 8 mm (⅓ inch) thick. **THREE** Arrange the vegetables and duck on a large plate. Stir 2 teaspoons salt and the sake into the stock and transfer to an ovenproof earthenware pot (*donabe*) or a heavy-based pot. Bring the stock to the boil over a table cooker at the dining table. Prepare 4 dipping bowls for your guests. **FOUR** Put the cabbage, leek and mushrooms into the stock, but the duck and mizuna are cooked as you eat. Each diner pours a little sauce into a bowl and mixes it with some stock from the pot. The food is scooped from the pot into the diner's bowl and eaten with the sauce, with Japanese pepper sprinkled over for a spicier taste.

Serves 4

NUTRIENT ANALYSIS PER SERVING 1867 kJ – 450 cal – 15 g protein – 7 g carbohydrate – 5 g sugars – 40 g fat – 11 g saturated fat – 3 g fibre – 1170 mg sodium

HEALTHY TIP Orange juice goes well with duck and is high in vitamin C and folate. Vitamin C is essential for the maintenance of healthy connective tissue, and folate is essential for cell formation and growth.

Stir-fried pork in ginger sauce *Kawari shoga yaki*

Stir-fried potatoes taste quite different from baked or boiled potatoes, and they add an interesting texture to this pork dish.

INGREDIENTS *450 g (14½ oz) lean pork, thinly sliced* ‖ *½ onion, thinly sliced* ‖ *450 g (14½ oz) potatoes, cut into matchsticks then soaked in water* ‖ *2 tablespoons vegetable oil* ‖ *6 shiso or Thai basil leaves, shredded* ‖ *rice, to serve*

MARINADE *juice from 2.5 cm (1 inch) fresh root ginger, peeled, grated and squeezed* ‖ *2 tablespoons shoyu* ‖ *2 tablespoons sake* ‖ *2 tablespoons mirin* ‖ *1 teaspoon rice vinegar*

ONE Make the marinade by mixing together all the ingredients. Put the pork and onion into a non-metallic dish, pour over the marinade and leave to marinate for 30 minutes. **TWO** Drain the potatoes and rinse them under running water. Drain thoroughly. **THREE** Heat 1 tablespoon oil in a nonstick frying pan and fry the potatoes over a moderate heat for 5–7 minutes or until they are soft and translucent. Transfer them to a plate. **FOUR** Add the remaining oil to the pan and fry the pork, onion and marinade until the pork is cooked. Mix in the potatoes and cook for a further 2 minutes. **FIVE** Stir in the shiso leaves and remove from the heat. Serve warm on a plate with a bowl of rice.

Serves 4

NUTRIENT ANALYSIS PER SERVING 1369 kJ – 327 cal – 27 g protein – 22 g carbohydrate – 2 g sugars – 14 g fat – 3 g saturated fat – 2 g fibre – 526 mg sodium

HEALTHY TIP Ginger has been credited for improving circulation, and over many years has been used to combat nausea and stomach cramps.

Crispy grilled liver

Leba yaki Roasted sesame seeds bring crispiness to this dish, in which the brandy and miso marinade cut through the dense flavour of the liver.

INGREDIENTS *450 g (14½ oz) pigs' or lambs' liver, cut into 8 mm (⅓ inch) slices* ‖ *4 tablespoons roasted white sesame seeds* ‖ *2 tablespoons arrowroot* ‖ *1 teaspoon salt* ‖ *4 tablespoons roasted black sesame seeds*

BRANDY AND MISO MARINADE *1 tablespoon brandy* ‖ *1 teaspoon lemon juice* ‖ *2 tablespoons miso* ‖ *2 tablespoons mirin* ‖ *1 garlic clove, crushed*

TO SERVE *green salad* ‖ *roasted sesame oil*

ONE Make the marinade by mixing together all the ingredients. Put the liver in a non-metallic dish, pour over the marinade, transfer to the refrigerator and leave for 18–48 hours. **TWO** Mix the white sesame seeds with 1 tablespoon arrowroot and ½ teaspoon salt on a small plate. Repeat with the black sesame seeds. **THREE** Wipe the liver with kitchen paper. Roll half the liver in the white sesame mixture and coat evenly. Roll the other half in the black sesame mixture. **FOUR** Lightly oil a baking sheet and arrange the sesame-coated liver on it. Cook under a preheated moderate grill for 7–8 minutes, turning once. Do not overcook. **FIVE** Serve warm with a simple green salad tossed with a little sesame oil.

Serves 4

NUTRIENT ANALYSIS PER SERVING 1643 kJ – 394 cal – 28 g protein – 9 g carbohydrate – 1 g sugars – 26 g fat – 5 g saturated fat – 0 g fibre – 850 mg sodium

HEALTHY TIP Liver is a particularly good source of iron in the diet and is also high in the fat-soluble vitamins A and D. Pregnant women should not eat large amounts of liver because the high vitamin A content could cause damage to the developing child.

Spicy chicken

Tori no koshou yaki This is a dish for lovers of spicy foods. The sansho and peppercorns form a crust that sparkles on the tongue.

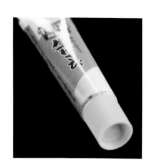

INGREDIENTS *450 g (14½ oz) chicken breast (with skins)* ‖ *1 tablespoon sake* ‖ *1 teaspoon salt* ‖ *1 teaspoon cracked mixed peppercorns* ‖ *1 teaspoon sansho (Japanese pepper) or ground white pepper* ‖ *1 tablespoon lime, lemon or orange rind* ‖ *2 tablespoons roasted sesame oil*

DRESSING *2 tablespoons rice vinegar* ‖ *4 tablespoons vegetable oil* ‖ *1 teaspoon wasabi* ‖ *½ teaspoon salt*

SALAD *250 g (8 oz) mixed young green salad leaves, cucumber and chicory*

ONE Pierce the chicken all over with a fork or a skewer and put in a plastic bag. Add the sake and salt and turn until the chicken is coated. Leave to marinate for 30 minutes. **TWO** Coat the chicken with the peppercorns, sansho and citrus rind, pressing them firmly into the meat. **THREE** Heat the oil in a nonstick frying pan and add the chicken, skin side down. Press the meat down and cook over a moderate heat for about 5 minutes or until the skin is crisp. Turn over the chicken and cook it, covered, over a low heat for a further 10–15 minutes. When the meat is almost cooked, remove the lid and finish off the cooking. Leave the meat to cool slightly, then cut it into 2.5 cm (1 inch) squares. **FOUR** Meanwhile, make the dressing by mixing together all the ingredients. Prepare the salad by cutting the leaves into 1 cm (½ inch) strips and mixing them together. **FIVE** Serve the chicken hot with the salad and dressing.

Serves 4

NUTRIENT ANALYSIS PER SERVING 1750 kJ – 423 cal – 21 g protein – 2 g carbohydrate – 2 g sugars – 37 g fat – 9 g saturated fat – 1 g fibre – 812 mg sodium

HEALTHY TIP Salad leaves, cucumber and chicory are good sources of vitamins, especially of folate which is essential for cell formation and growth.

Steak with rice tubes *Wafu steki to kiritanpo*

Rice tubes (*kiritanpo*) are widely eaten in northern Japan, where they are often grilled and added to a hotpot of game bird and wild herbs. In this dish the tubes accompany teriyaki-style steak to make a filling meal.

INGREDIENTS *480 g (15½ oz) freshly cooked white rice (see page 17)* ‖ *⅓ teaspoon salt* ‖ *vegetable oil, for brushing* ‖ *2 long, slim aubergines or 1 large, round aubergine, cut lengthways into 5 mm (¼ inch) slices* ‖ *1 red pepper, deseeded and cut lengthways into 5 mm (¼ inch) slices* ‖ *1 green pepper, deseeded and cut lengthways into 5 mm (¼ inch) slices* ‖ *8 green asparagus spears, blanched* ‖ *600 g (1¼ lb) sirloin steak* ‖ *4 garlic cloves, roughly chopped* ‖ *3 teaspoons shoyu* ‖ *1 tablespoon sake* ‖ *salt and cracked white pepper* ‖ *4 chives, to garnish* ‖ *1 lemon, cut into 8 wedges, to serve*

ONE Put the rice in a bowl and use a fork to mash it to a sticky mush. Add the salt and divide the rice into 8. Spread a portion on a piece of clingfilm on a rolling mat, place a lightly oiled chopstick 2.5 cm (1 inch) from the front edge of the rice and wrap it tightly into a 10 cm (4 inch) long tube. Remove the chopstick and place the tube on a lightly oiled baking sheet. Repeat the process to make 8 rice tubes. **TWO** Brush the aubergine and pepper slices and the asparagus with oil. Cook the rice and vegetables on a griddle or under a preheated hot grill until the rice is golden-brown and the vegetables are brown. **THREE** Put the steak in a frying pan, sprinkle it with a little salt and coat the surface with garlic and cracked white pepper. Cook the steak until it is cooked as you like and, just before you remove it from the heat, add the shoyu, which will burn as it meets the edge of the pan. Transfer the meat to a warm plate and, just before serving, cut it into 2 cm (¾ inch) slices. **FOUR** Add the sake to the frying pan and heat, stirring, for 1 minute. Reserve the liquid as a sauce. **FIVE** Arrange the rice tubes and vegetables on a plate, then add the steak. Spoon over the sauce and garnish with chives. Serve immediately with lemon wedges.

Serves 4

NUTRIENT ANALYSIS PER SERVING 1795 kJ – 426 cal – 41 g protein – 43 g carbohydrate – 5 g sugars – 11 g fat – 3 g saturated fat – 5 g fibre – 880 mg sodium

HEALTHY TIP The rice and vegetables in this dish provide an excellent source of energy and fibre to complement the good-quality protein of the steak.

Vegetables and mushrooms wrapped in pork *Yasai no niku maki*

Only a small amount of meat is used in this dish, but the wrapped vegetables soak up the flavour and make this a satisfying and filling meal.

INGREDIENTS *2 carrots, cut lengthways into 5 mm (¼ inch) square sticks* ‖ *8 slices of pork loin or rashers of unsmoked bacon* ‖ *125 g (4 oz) enoki mushrooms, cleaned* ‖ *8 green asparagus spears* ‖ *1 tablespoon vegetable oil* ‖ *salt and pepper*

SWEET CHILLI SAUCE *3 tablespoons rice vinegar* ‖ *3 tablespoons caster sugar* ‖ *3 tablespoons water* ‖ *1 garlic clove, finely chopped* ‖ *1 dried chilli, finely crushed* ‖ *1 teaspoon paprika* ‖ *1½ teaspoons shoyu* ‖ *½ teaspoon arrowroot*

ONE Blanch the carrots in salted water for 2 minutes, drain and leave to cool. **TWO** Lay a slice of pork or rasher of bacon on a chopping board and add one-eighth of the mushroom, two carrot sticks and 1 asparagus spear. Roll this up in the pork or bacon. Repeat this to make 8 rolls. Sprinkle with salt and pepper (omit the salt if you are using bacon). **THREE** Heat the oil in a nonstick frying pan, add the rolls, seam side down, and cook gently for 5–6 minutes. **FOUR** Make the sauce by mixing together all the ingredients (except the arrowroot). Blend the arrowroot with ½ teaspoon water and stir it into the sauce until it thickens. **FIVE** Cut each roll in half and arrange the pieces on 4 plates. Serve warm with the sauce.

Serves 4

NUTRIENT ANALYSIS PER SERVING 866 kJ – 206 cal – 15 g protein – 21 g carbohydrate – 20 g sugars – 8 g fat – 2 g saturated fat – 2 g fibre – 160 mg sodium

HEALTHY TIP Mushrooms provide useful amounts of some of the B vitamins and also contain copper. Copper is a trace mineral necessary for the enzymes involved in bone growth and the formation of connective tissue.

Simmered beef with vegetables *Niku jyaga*

Slow-simmered dishes are the epitome of traditional Japanese home cooking, and they are sometimes described as the 'taste of mother'. This popular dish can be made well in advance of serving. To make slicing easier, put the meat in the freezer for 2–3 hours, but don't allow it to become too hard.

INGREDIENTS *250 g (8 oz) shirataki (yam noodles)* ‖ *2 tablespoons vegetable oil* ‖ *200 g (7 oz) beef steak, cut into thin ribbons* ‖ *1 large onion, sliced* ‖ *700 g (1 lb 7 oz) new potatoes, whole or cut in half if large* ‖ *1 carrot, cut into thick slices* ‖ *1 tablespoon sake* ‖ *1 tablespoon caster sugar* ‖ *2 tablespoons shoyu* ‖ *1 tablespoon mirin* ‖ *3 tablespoons blanched green peas (fresh or frozen)* ‖ *rice, to serve*

ONE Put the noodles in a sieve and pour over plenty of hot water from a just-boiled kettle. Drain and cut the noodles into 5–8 cm (2–3 inch) lengths. **TWO** Heat the oil in a heavy-based pan over a moderate heat and fry the meat and onion until the meat changes colour. Gather the meat into the centre of the pan. Add the noodles, potatoes and carrot. **THREE** Mix together the sake, sugar, shoyu and mirin and pour the mixture over the meat. Wait for 1 minute and pour 300 ml (½ pint) water over the meat. Simmer, covered, for 10–15 minutes or until the potatoes and carrot are cooked but not too soft. **FOUR** Add the peas and remove from the heat. Serve hot with a bowl of rice.

Serves 4

NUTRIENT ANALYSIS PER SERVING 1304 kJ – 310 cal – 15 g protein – 44 g carbohydrate – 13 g sugars – 9 g fat – 2 g saturated fat – 7 g fibre – 58 mg sodium

HEALTHY TIP Shirataki are gelatinous noodles made from the starch of a type of yam potato. They are rich in fibre and have few calories and are widely used in dishes for dieters in Japan as well as in traditional dishes.

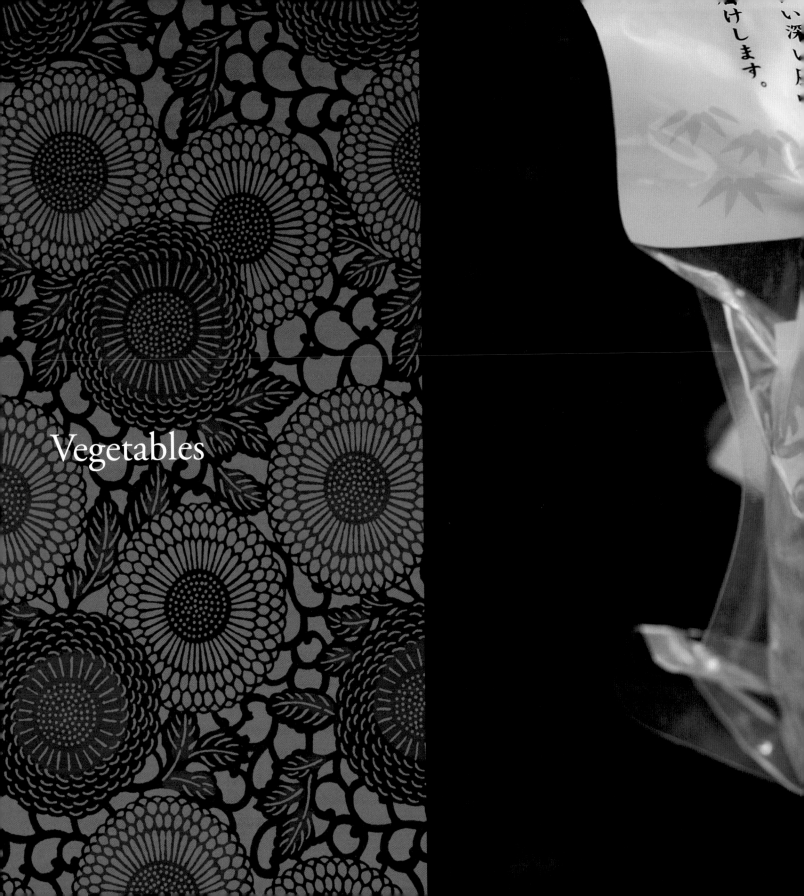

Vegetables

Tofu, wakame and spring onion salad *Aggé to negi no yohu nuta* This delicious salad was inspired by a *yakuzen* menu, which includes dishes specially prepared for medicinal purposes. Saikyo miso paste is less salty than ordinary miso; if you use ordinary miso paste omit the salt.

INGREDIENTS *4 spring onions, cut into 3 cm (1¼ inch) pieces* ‖ *5 g (¼ oz) dried wakame, soaked in water for 5 minutes* ‖ *2 abura age* ‖ *2–3 sprigs of watercress, to garnish*

DRESSING *5 teaspoons rice vinegar* ‖ *3 tablespoons vegetable oil* ‖ *1 teaspoon caster sugar* ‖ *1 tablespoon saikyo miso paste* ‖ *½ teaspoon salt* ‖ *white pepper*

ONE In a small saucepan boil the spring onions in water for 1 minute, then add the drained wakame. Cook for a further minute. Drain into a sieve held under cold running water. Drain well and leave to cool. **TWO** Put the abura age in a sieve and pour hot water over it to wash off the oil absorbed by the tofu. Squeeze the water out with your hands when it has cooled. Cook them under a preheated moderate grill, turning once, until both sides are crisp, then cut them into 5 mm x 2.5 cm (¼ x 1 inch) pieces. **THREE** Make the dressing by mixing together all the ingredients. Whisk well to blend. **FOUR** Mix the wakame, spring onions and abura age pieces with the dressing in a bowl. Garnish with watercress leaves and serve.

Serves 4

NUTRIENT ANALYSIS PER SERVING 569 kJ – 137 cal – 5 g protein – 3 g carbohydrate – 2 g sugars – 12 g fat – 1 g saturated fat – 0 g fibre – 470 mg sodium

HEALTHY TIP Spring onions contain lutein and zeazanthin, which may have a role in the prevention of macular degeneration in the eyes.

Grilled shiitake mushrooms with orange sauce

Shiitake no mikan ae Shiitake mushrooms have a distinctive earthy aroma, which some people find rather overpowering. The orange sauce neutralizes the scent of the mushrooms, making it possible for everyone to enjoy their *umami* (flavour).

INGREDIENTS *250 g (8 oz) shiitake mushrooms, stalks removed* ‖ *2 teaspoons vegetable oil* ‖ *2 tablespoons sake or dry sherry* ‖ *1 spring onion, finely chopped* ‖ *3 tablespoons shoyu* ‖ *3 tablespoons orange juice* ‖ *5 g (¼ oz) kezuri bushi (dried bonito flakes)* ‖ *2 teaspoons slivers of orange rind, to garnish*

ONE Cut a shallow cross in the top of each shiitake. Heat the oil in a nonstick frying pan and put the mushrooms in the pan, one by one, cap side up. Cook over a medium heat for 2 minutes, then turn them over. **TWO** Sprinkle the sake over the mushrooms. Reduce the heat to low and cook, covered, for 5 minutes. Turn over the mushrooms again. **THREE** Mix together the spring onion, shoyu and orange juice. Pour the mixture over the mushrooms and remove the pan from the heat. Re-cover and leave to marinate for 5 minutes. **FOUR** Arrange the mushrooms on a large plate and sprinkle over the kezuri bushi (omit if vegetarian). Garnish with slivers of orange rind and serve warm.

Serves 4 as a side dish

NUTRIENT ANALYSIS PER SERVING 180 kJ – 43 cal – 3 g protein – 2 g carbohydrate – 1 g sugars – 2 g fat – 0 g saturated fat – 1 g fibre – 650 mg sodium

HEALTHY TIP Mushrooms are eaten mostly for their flavour, and are not high in many nutrients. The orange juice in the sauce in this dish adds vitamin C, some folate and some calcium.

Simmered yams
Satoimo no nimono The word *nimono* means stewed foods, which have long been a staple of Japanese cooking. This is a traditional dish, which has been enjoyed by generations in Japan.

INGREDIENTS *600 g (1¼ lb) satoimo yams, washed* ‖ *5 tablespoons umeshu (plum wine)* ‖ *5 tablespoons shoyu* ‖ *1 tablespoon sake* ‖ *12 baby carrots* ‖ *250 g (8 oz) fine French beans* ‖ *rind of ¼ yuzu (Japanese citrus fruit) or lime, shredded*

ONE Cut off the top and bottom of each yam, then remove the skin, peeling thickly. The juice is rather slimy, so plunge each yam into a bowl of water as you peel it. Place the peeled yams in a sieve or strainer and wash under running water for a few minutes. **TWO** Put the rinsed, peeled yams in a steamer and cook for about 20 minutes or until tender. **THREE** Mix together the umeshu, shoyu and sake in a medium-sized, heavy-based pan and add 200 ml (7 fl oz) water. Add the carrots and bring to the boil. Reduce the heat and add the yams. Simmer over a low heat for 10 minutes, shaking the pan gently from time to time. **FOUR** Boil the beans in salted water for 3–4 minutes, then add them to the pan. Remove the pan from the heat, sprinkle over the citrus rind and serve hot.

Serves 4 as a side dish

NUTRIENT ANALYSIS PER SERVING 990 kJ – 233 cal – 6 g protein – 50 g carbohydrate – 6 g sugars – 1 g fat – 0 g saturated fat – 9 g fibre – 1100 mg sodium

HEALTHY TIP Yams are high in dietary fibre, essential for maintaining good bowel health and in the prevention of bowel cancer.

Stuffed pumpkin *Mushi kabocha sasage zume* This warming dish is ideal for

a cold winter's day. Although yellow miso paste is traditionally used, you can use any other type of miso if you prefer. If you cannot find a kabocha pumpkin use an ordinary pumpkin, about 20 cm (8 inches) across.

INGREDIENTS *1 kabocha pumpkin* ‖ *230 g (7½ oz) dried sasage or aduki beans or 2 x 425 g (14 oz) cans aduki beans* ‖ *2 teaspoons vegetable oil* ‖ *2 garlic cloves, crushed* ‖ *2.5 cm (1 inch) fresh root ginger, peeled and grated or finely chopped* ‖ *1 red onion, finely chopped* ‖ *50 g (2 oz) dried pumpkin seeds* ‖ *1 tablespoon black sesame seeds* ‖ *2 tablespoons shoyu* ‖ *2 teaspoons plain flour* ‖ *wholemeal breadcrumbs (optional)*

SAUCE *4 tablespoons yellow miso paste* ‖ *2 tablespoons Dashi Stock (see page 19) or water* ‖ *1 tablespoon mirin* ‖ *pinch of nutmeg*

ONE Cut the top off the pumpkin and remove all seeds to create a hollow bowl. **TWO** If you are using dried beans, cook them *(see page 12)*. Drain and mash the beans with a fork. **THREE** Heat the oil in a small, nonstick frying pan and cook the garlic, ginger and onion until soft. Combine the onion mixture with the beans, pumpkin seeds, sesame seeds and shoyu. **FOUR** Sprinkle flour inside the pumpkin and fill it with the bean mixture. If the pumpkin is large and there is more than 5 cm (2 inches) space at the top, mix some wholemeal breadcrumbs into the stuffing. **FIVE** Pour water into a large roasting pan to a depth of 5 cm (2 inches), add the pumpkin and bake in a preheated oven, 240°C (475°F), Gas Mark 9, for 45–60 minutes. When the pumpkin is cooked a skewer will pierce the side easily. Turn off the heat and keep the pumpkin warm in the oven. **SIX** Meanwhile, make the sauce by whisking together all the ingredients in a small saucepan. Heat gently, stirring constantly, until the surface starts to bubble. Cut the pumpkin into 6–8 segments and serve with the warm sauce.

Serves 6–8 as a main dish

NUTRIENT ANALYSIS PER SERVING 1025 kJ – 243 cal – 14 g protein – 32 g carbohydrate – 5 g sugars – 7 g fat – 1 g saturated fat – 6 g fibre – 790 mg sodium

HEALTHY TIP Most red and yellow fleshed vegetables and fruits have a high carotene content, but pumpkin has only a moderate carotene content.

Five vegetable pickle

Gomoku yasai zuke Pickles are an indispensable element in Japanese cooking. Use these vitamin-packed pickles as an accompaniment for freshly cooked rice or eat them as a salad. The vegetables will keep for up to a week in the refrigerator.

INGREDIENTS *100 g (3½ oz) salad radishes* ‖ *200 g (7 oz) cucumber* ‖ *100 g (3½ oz) carrot, peeled and cut into ribbons* ‖ *50 g (2 oz) broccoli stem, peeled and thinly sliced* ‖ *1 small apple, cored and thinly sliced* ‖ *2.5 cm (1 inch) fresh root ginger, peeled and cut into thin strips* ‖ *1 small, dried chilli, deseeded and finely chopped* ‖ *1 tablespoon cider vinegar* ‖ *piece of konbu (kelp), 5 cm (2 inches) square, cut into 1 x 2.5 cm (½ x 1 inch) pieces* ‖ *1 teaspoon salt*

ONE Wrap the radish and cucumber together in a tea towel and crush them roughly with a rolling pin. **TWO** Put all the ingredients in a plastic bag. Remove as much air as possible and tie the opening. Knead the bag with your hands so that the vegetables are coated and leave in the refrigerator for at least 30 minutes or overnight. **THREE** Serve the pickles with rice or a rice dish. Alternatively, eat the mixed vegetables as a salad, but soak them in water for 1 hour, then drain and mix with 1 teaspoon vegetable oil and 1 teaspoon apple vinegar.

Serves 4

NUTRIENT ANALYSIS PER SERVING 128 kJ – 30 cal – 2 g protein – 6 g carbohydrate – 5 g sugars – 0 g fat – 0 g saturated fat – 2 g fibre – 544 mg sodium

HEALTHY TIP Broccoli, like most dark green vegetables, is a very good source of folate, which is important for cell formation and growth, and therefore particularly valuable in the early stages of pregnancy.

Cucumber and seaweed salad *Kyuri to kaiso sunomono* Seaweed

should really be known as sea vegetable and enjoy greater popularity outside of Japan because of its amazing anti-ageing properties.

INGREDIENTS *1 teaspoon salt* ‖ *2 small cucumbers, thinly sliced* ‖ *5 g (¼ oz) mixed dried seaweed, such as wakame, dulse, kelp, arame, sea spaghetti, kanten and carrageen (Irish moss), soaked in warm water for 10 minutes and drained* ‖ *2.5 cm (1 inch) fresh root ginger, peeled and cut into thin strips*

DRESSING *3 tablespoons rice vinegar* ‖ *1 tablespoon caster sugar* ‖ *1 tablespoon Dashi Stock (see page 19)* ‖ *1 teaspoon shoyu* ‖ *1 teaspoon roasted white sesame seeds* ‖ *1 teaspoon Japanese or English mustard*

ONE Sprinkle the salt over the cucumber slices and leave them to soften for 10 minutes. Rinse and drain. **TWO** Cut the seaweed into bite-sized pieces if necessary and squeeze out any excess water. **THREE** Mix together all the ingredients for the dressing in a bowl. **FOUR** Just before serving, mix the cucumber slices, seaweed and ginger in a bowl and serve, with the dressing, at room temperature as an accompaniment for both meat and fish dishes.

Serves 4 as a side dish

NUTRIENT ANALYSIS PER SERVING 160 kJ – 38 cal – 1 g protein – 7 g carbohydrate – 6 g sugars – 1 g fat – 0 g saturated fat – 0 g fibre – 570 mg sodium

HEALTHY TIP This refreshing salad and fat-free dressing are not only extremely low in calories but are also nutritious, containing many beneficial minerals, which help to maintain healthy skin and hair.

Hakusai, cottage cheese and goji berry salad *Hakusai to kukonomi salada*

Goji berries, *kukonomi*, have been eaten in China for over 4,000 years and are an important ingredient in *yakuzen* (healthy) diets. Also known as wolfberries, they are available from health-food and oriental stores.

INGREDIENTS *2 tablespoons dried kukonomi (goji berries), soaked in warm water for 5 minutes* ‖ *1 nashi pear, peeled, cored, quartered and sliced* ‖ *⅛ hakusai (Chinese cabbage), thickly sliced* ‖ *bunch of mitsuba leaves or a handful of mizuna leaves, roughly chopped* ‖ *5 tablespoons cottage cheese*

DRESSING *1 spring onion (white part only), finely chopped* ‖ *2 tablespoons toasted sesame oil* ‖ *2 tablespoons rice vinegar* ‖ *1 tablespoon honey* ‖ *½ teaspoon salt* ‖ *1 tablespoon white Suri Goma (see page 20)* ‖ *pinch of chilli pepper*

ONE Make the dressing by whisking together all the ingredients. Transfer to the refrigerator until required.

TWO Drain the berries and mix them gently in a salad bowl with the pear, cabbage and mitsuba leaves.

THREE Just before serving, pour the dressing over the vegetables. Fold together quickly and top with cottage cheese. Serve cold.

Serves 4 as a side dish

NUTRIENT ANALYSIS PER SERVING 640 kJ – 150 cal – 8 g protein – 10 g carbohydrate – 10 g sugars – 9 g fat – 2 g saturated fat – 1 g fibre – 448 mg sodium

HEALTHY TIP Cottage cheese is low in fat, and is an excellent source of protein and calcium. Goji berries have a high carotene content, so are a useful anti-oxidant.

Stir-fried bean sprouts and chilli *Moyashi itame* Inexpensive

and versatile, bean sprouts are a popular ingredient in Japanese cooking. This is a quick and easy dish for a busy day, and if you wish you can use a vegetarian 'oyster' sauce made from mushrooms.

INGREDIENTS *2 tablespoons roasted sesame oil* ‖ *1 garlic clove, finely chopped* ‖ *1 cm (½ inch) fresh root ginger, peeled and finely chopped* ‖ *1 small, dried chilli, deseeded and finely chopped* ‖ *400 g (13 oz) bean sprouts, washed* (see page 12) ‖ *250 g (8 oz) green asparagus spears, cut in half lengthways and sliced diagonally* ‖ *50 g (2 oz) shiitake mushrooms, thinly sliced* ‖ *50 g (2 oz) carrot, cut into strips* ‖ *1 tablespoon arrowroot or cornflour* ‖ *rice, to serve*

SEASONINGS *2 tablespoons mirin* ‖ *1 tablespoon red miso paste* ‖ *1 tablespoon soy sauce* ‖ *2 teaspoons Chinese chilli bean paste* ‖ *1 teaspoon oyster sauce*

ONE Mix together the seasonings with 200 ml (7 fl oz) water and set aside until required. **TWO** Heat the sesame oil in a wok or a large, nonstick frying pan over a high heat and fry the garlic, ginger and chilli for 1 minute. Add all the vegetables to the pan. Toss gently for 3 minutes, then add the mixed seasonings. Cook for a further 2 minutes. **THREE** Mix the arrowroot with 1 tablespoon water. Stir it into the vegetables, mix well and remove from the heat when the liquid has thickened. Serve immediately with a bowl of rice.

Serves 4

NUTRIENT ANALYSIS PER SERVING 596 kJ – 143 cal – 8 g protein – 13 g carbohydrate – 3 g sugars – 7 g fat – 1 g saturated fat – 2 g fibre – 660 mg sodium

HEALTHY TIP Bean sprouts provide a pleasant crunchy texture and contain small amounts of most of the B vitamins.

Grilled bamboo shoot with herb cream *Yaki takenoko*

This combination of a bamboo shoot and a peppery green dressing evokes the spring wind, which is traditionally regarded as having the power to restart everything afresh.

INGREDIENTS *1 whole boiled takenoko (bamboo shoot)* ‖ *50 ml (2 fl oz) shoyu* ‖ *1½ tablespoon mirin* ‖ *½ teaspoon sansho (Japanese pepper) or ground green peppercorns*

HERB CREAM *50 g (2 oz) watercress leaves, reserve a handful for garnish, finely chopped* ‖ *3 tablespoons plain yogurt* ‖ *1 tablespoon mayonnaise* ‖ *1 teaspoon shoyu*

ONE Cut the bamboo shoot into 8 pieces lengthways. Mix together the shoyu, mirin and sansho and marinate the bamboo shoot for 10 minutes. **TWO** Make the herb cream. Reserving 1 leaf for garnish, roughly pound the kinome leaves and watercress together with a pestle and mortar, then mix the leaves with the yogurt, mayonnaise and shoyu. Alternatively, blend all the ingredients in a food processor. Set aside. **THREE** Cook the bamboo shoot under a preheated moderate grill for 7–10 minutes or in a griddle, turning it every few minutes and brushing the surface with the marinade to avoid burning. Remove from the heat when the edges are crisp. Serve the bamboo shoot warm with the cream dressing and garnished with the reserved watercress leaves.

Serves 4 as a side dish

NUTRIENT ANALYSIS PER SERVING 409 kJ – 99 cal – 4 g protein – 4 g carbohydrate – 3 g sugars – 7 g fat – 1 g saturated fat – 2 g fibre – 930 mg sodium

HEALTHY TIP Watercress is high in calcium and also in folate. Much of the folate content of vegetables can be lost in cooking, so a raw source of the vitamin is useful.

Lotus root and black beans in curry sauce *Renkon to kuromame kare fumi*

The contrasts of colour and texture make this a particularly appetizing dish, which is an excellent accompaniment for beer or sake. Black kidney beans are available in oriental shops. If wished, replace the Worcestershire sauce with any of the similar brown sauces that are suitable for vegetarians.

INGREDIENTS *80 g (3¼ oz) dried black or red kidney beans or 200 g (7 oz) cooked beans, drained* ‖ *1 teaspoon baking soda (see step 1)* ‖ *300 g (10 oz) renkon (lotus root)* ‖ *50 ml (2 fl oz) rice vinegar* ‖ *3 tablespoons vegetable oil* ‖ *rice, to serve*

CURRY SAUCE *200 ml (7 fl oz) Dashi Stock (see page 19)* ‖ *1 garlic clove, crushed* ‖ *1 tablespoon Worcestershire sauce* ‖ *1 tablespoon tomato paste* ‖ *3 tablespoons shoyu* ‖ *1 tablespoon mirin* ‖ *1 teaspoon honey* ‖ *½ tablespoon mild curry powder*

ONE If you are using dried beans, wash and cover them with piping hot water. Add ½ teaspoon baking soda and leave at room temperature overnight. Rinse and boil the beans in the fresh water for 3–4 hours over a low heat until they are soft. **TWO** Make the curry sauce by mixing together all the ingredients in a medium-sized, heavy-based saucepan. Bring to the boil, add the cooked beans and simmer for 15 minutes. **THREE** Peel the lotus root. Add the vinegar to a saucepan with 600 ml (1 pint) water and cook the lotus root until it is tender. Cut it into slices 5 mm (¼ inch) thick and dry them on kitchen paper. **FOUR** Heat the oil in a nonstick frying pan and fry the slices, in batches, until the edges are golden. Remove them from the oil and drain on kitchen paper. **FIVE** Add the lotus root slices to the beans. Cook for a further 5 minutes over a low heat, then leave for the flavours to infuse for at least 1 hour. **SIX** Serve warm with some rice. This dish may be eaten cold as a starter.

Serves 4

NUTRIENT ANALYSIS PER SERVING 879 kJ – 210 cal – 7 g protein – 22 g carbohydrate – 8 g sugars – 11 g fat – 1 g saturated fat – 6 g fibre – 1118 mg sodium

HEALTHY TIP If using kidney beans they must be cooked in fast boiling water for at least 10 minutes before slow cooking.

Stewed cold aubergines *Nasu no hiyashi ni* This recipe is based on a traditional dish from the Kyoto region, and the glossy skins of the aubergines contain meltingly soft flesh. Long, slim aubergines are best, but if you cannot find them use 4 large, oval ones instead.

INGREDIENTS *8 long, slim aubergines* ‖ *2 tablespoons vegetable oil* ‖ *2 garlic cloves, sliced thinly* ‖ *3 okra*

SOUP *800 ml (28 fl oz) Dashi Stock (see page 19)* ‖ *3 tablespoons sake* ‖ *½ tablespoon mirin* ‖ *3½ tablespoons shoyu* ‖ *pinch of salt*

ONE Trim the stems from the aubergines and score the skin lengthways with a sharp knife. Leave them in a bowl of water for 10 minutes to remove the bitter juice from the skin. **TWO** Arrange the aubergines in a single layer in a large, heavy-based saucepan with a tight-fitting lid. **THREE** Mix together the ingredients for the soup and pour the mixture over the aubergines. Bring to the boil, reduce the heat to low and cover the aubergines with a circle of greaseproof paper that just fits inside the pan. Cover and cook for 20 minutes. Pierce the aubergines with a skewer; if it goes in smoothly, they may be removed from the heat. Leave the aubergines to cool in the soup. Once cool, keep them in the refrigerator for at least 3 hours or overnight. **FOUR** Heat the oil in a small, nonstick frying pan and cook the garlic slices until they are crisp and golden. Drain the garlic on kitchen paper and set aside. **FIVE** Cook the okra in boiling water for 3 minutes and cut them into 1 cm (½ inch) pieces. **SIX** Pile the aubergines into a large serving bowl and pour some soup over the top, discarding any soup that is not needed. Garnish the aubergines with okra and garlic chips and serve cold with a rice dish, such as Redbush Tea Pilaf with Walnuts *(see page 134)*.

Serves 4

NUTRIENT ANALYSIS PER SERVING 522 kJ – 124 cal – 5 g protein – 9 g carbohydrate – 7 g sugars – 7 g fat – 1 g saturated fat – 8 g fibre – 809 mg sodium (not including added salt)

HEALTHY TIP Aubergines look beautiful and have a pleasant flavour, but are not particularly high in nutrients. Their main culinary advantage is that they absorb liquids, particularly oil, very easily. In this recipe there is little fat, so the total calorie count is low.

Stewed turnips with miso nuts

Kabu no furohuki The gently cooked turnips are filled with richly flavoured nuts. You can use the flesh you scoop out of the turnips in a salad or stir-fried dish.

INGREDIENTS *8 medium or 12 small turnips* ‖ *1 litre (1¾ pints) Dashi Stock (see page 19)* ‖ *2 teaspoons shoyu* ‖ *250 g (8 oz) spinach*

MISO NUTS *3 tablespoons brown or white miso* ‖ *1 tablespoon mirin* ‖ *1½ tablespoons sake* ‖ *50 g (2 oz) mixed unsalted nuts, chopped* ‖ *1 tablespoon grated Parmesan cheese*

ONE Peel the turnips, cut off the tops and scoop out the flesh to make hollow cups with lids. **TWO** Put the stock in a saucepan, bring to the boil and add the shoyu and turnip cups. Simmer over a low heat until the turnips are translucent. Remove the cups, place them upside down on a plate and keep them warm. **THREE** Blanch the spinach in the remaining stock for 1 minute, drain and squeeze out any excess liquid. **FOUR** Prepare the nuts. In a saucepan mix together the miso, mirin and sake. Heat, stirring constantly, until the mixture is smooth and shiny. Remove from the heat and stir in the nuts and cheese. **FIVE** Fill the turnip cups with the nuts and cook under a preheated hot grill until the surface is bubbling. Put the lids on the turnip cups, arrange them over a bed of spinach and serve immediately.

Serves 4

NUTRIENT ANALYSIS PER SERVING 766 kJ – 182 cal – 10 g protein – 15 g carbohydrate – 13 g sugars – 9 g fat – 2 g saturated fat – 11 g fibre – 1288 mg sodium

HEALTHY TIP Turnips are a good source of dietary fibre, and also contain vitamin C. Peel turnips thinly and boil for as short a time as possible to preserve the vitamin C content.

Rice and noodles

Brown rice with mushrooms and edamame *Kinoko genmai gohan*

Kinoko genmai gohan The brown rice and mushrooms provide extra flavour, while the freshly boiled edamade bring a contrasting crunchiness to this dish. Edamame, fresh soya beans in their shells, are available frozen in the West.

INGREDIENTS *540 g (1 lb 3 oz) short grain brown rice, washed and drained* ‖ *80 g (3¼ oz) mixed mushrooms, such as shiitake, oyster, enoki and shimeji* ‖ *50 ml (2 fl oz) shoyu* ‖ *1 tablespoon salt* ‖ *50 ml (2 fl oz) mirin* ‖ *150 g (5 oz) edamame (fresh soya beans in their shells)*

ONE Cook the brown rice in 1.2 litres (2 pints) water in a heavy-based pan with a tight-fitting lid. When the water has boiled, reduce the heat to a simmer. Cook until the bubbling noise subsides and a faint crackling noise starts. This takes 30–45 minutes. Remove from the heat and leave, without lifting the lid, until the other ingredients are ready. **TWO** Prepare the mushrooms. If you are using shiitake or oyster mushrooms cut them into thin strips. Cut enoki mushrooms into 2.5 cm (1 inch pieces). Separate the clusters of shimeji mushrooms. **THREE** Mix together the shoyu and mirin with 50 ml (2 fl oz) water in a saucepan and bring to the boil. Add the mushrooms and cook, covered, for 10 minutes over a low heat. Pour the contents of the pan into the rice and mix well with a rice paddle. Re-cover the saucepan. **FOUR** Add the salt to a saucepan of boiling water and cook the soya beans for 3–4 minutes. Transfer to a sieve and hold under cold running water for a few minutes. Drain well. Shell the beans and mix them into the rice. **FIVE** Serve warm in individual bowls with Clear Soup with Prawns *(see page 24)*

Serves 4–6

NUTRIENT ANALYSIS PER SERVING 2253 kJ – 530 cal – 13 g protein – 113 g carbohydrate – 3 g sugars – 5 g fat – 1 g saturated fat – 6 g fibre – 2179 mg sodium

HEALTHY TIP Brown rice has only had the outer husk removed, so it retains flavour and is higher in the important B vitamins thiamine, riboflavin and niacin than white rice. Brown rice also contains a useful level of vitamin E, vital for the body's anti-oxidant processing.

Udon noodles with fried tofu *Kitsune udon* This simple noodle

dish lets you savour the flavour of the individual ingredients, including the dashi stock. Udon noodles are thick, wide wheat noodles, which are often used in the same types of dish as buckwheat noodles.

INGREDIENTS *4 abura age* ‖ *2 tablespoons shoyu* ‖ *2 tablespoons caster sugar* ‖ *1 tablespoon mirin* ‖ *1½ teaspoons sake or dry sherry* ‖ *300 g (10 oz) dried or 600 g (1¼ lb) fresh udon noodles* ‖ *2 litres (3½ pints) Tsuyu, recipe A (see page 20)* ‖ *3 spring onions* ‖ *2 teaspoons lemon or lime rind, cut into slivers, to garnish* ‖ *shichimi togarashi (optional), to serve*

ONE Put the abura age in a bowl and cover them with just-boiled water. Leave to stand for 1 minute, then drain. Repeat the process to remove any residual oil. Squeeze the abura age gently and transfer them to a saucepan. **TWO** Add the shoyu, sugar, mirin, sake and 150 ml (½ pint) water to the saucepan with the abura age and bring to the boil. Reduce the heat to low and simmer until the liquid is almost gone. Turn the abura age from time to time while they are cooking. Remove from the heat and leave to cool until required. **THREE** Cook the noodles according to the instructions on the packet. Turn them into a sieve and hold under cold running water, turning the noodles with your hands until they are cold. Drain thoroughly. **FOUR** Put the tsuyu in a saucepan and heat but do not boil. Add the white part of the spring onions, sliced lengthways, and noodles to reheat them. Transfer the soup to 4 deep bowls with 1 abura age in each. Garnish with the slivered citrus rind and finely chopped green part of the spring onions. Serve immediately with a sprinkling of shichimi togarashi if a spicier taste is preferred.

Serves 4

NUTRIENT ANALYSIS PER SERVING 1859 kJ – 440 cal – 18 g protein – 71 g carbohydrate – 12 g sugars – 10 g fat – 0 g saturated fat – 5 g fibre – 2060 mg sodium

HEALTHY TIP Noodles are a good source of dietary fibre and, like spaghetti, are a slow-release carbohydrate, sustaining energy levels over a period of time.

Spaghetti with Japanese sauce

Wafu spaghetti Japanese cooks are good at adapting other countries' foods. Spaghetti first became popular more than 60 years ago and immediately started to spawn plenty of Italian-Japanese fusion dishes such as this one.

INGREDIENTS *1 tablespoon olive oil* ‖ *1 garlic clove, crushed* ‖ *1 small, dried red chilli, deseeded and chopped* ‖ *100 g (3½ oz) maitake or oyster mushroom, washed and roughly torn* ‖ *100 g (3½ oz) shiitake mushroom, stalks removed and caps sliced* ‖ *100 g (3½ oz) chestnut mushrooms, sliced* ‖ *2 tablespoons sake* ‖ *2 teaspoons shoyu* ‖ *400 g (13 oz) dried spaghetti* ‖ *15 g (½ oz) butter or margarine* ‖ *2 shiso leaves, cut into thin strips, or a handful of chopped flat leaf parsley, to garnish*

ONE Heat the oil in a large, nonstick frying pan, add the garlic and fry until golden. Add the chilli and all the mushrooms. Cook, stirring, for 2–3 minutes, then add the sake. Simmer until liquid comes out of mushrooms, then remove from the heat and stir in the shoyu. **TWO** Meanwhile, cook the spaghetti according to the instructions on the packet, drain and add to the frying pan. Mix in the butter or margarine. **THREE** Garnish with shiso leaves or parsley and serve immediately.

Serves 4

NUTRIENT ANALYSIS PER SERVING 1757 kJ – 415 cal – 14 g protein – 75 g carbohydrate – 4 g sugars – 8 g fat – 3 g saturated fat – 6 g fibre – 197 mg sodium

HEALTHY TIP Mushrooms are generally low in major nutrients and are eaten mainly for their flavour, but they do contain small amounts of the B vitamins and some trace metals, particularly copper. Copper is an essential component of some enzymes and is needed for bone growth and the formation of connective tissue.

Buckwheat noodles with Japanese pesto *Kawari soba*

Soba (buckwheat) has been eaten as a grain in Japan for at least 3,000 years, but buckwheat noodles appeared only about 700 years ago. Soba has become a synonym for all noodle dishes and continues to be the basis of many modern recipes, such as this one. If you can't find green shiso leaves, use Italian or Thai basil for the garnish instead.

INGREDIENTS *400 g (13 oz) dried soba (buckwheat) noodles*

PESTO *30 green shiso leaves* ‖ *100 g (3½ oz) rocket leaves* ‖ *40 g (1½ oz) pine nuts, roasted* ‖ *1 garlic clove, crushed* ‖ *100 ml (3½ fl oz) olive oil* ‖ *2 tablespoons brown miso paste*

ONE Reserve a few shiso and rocket leaves for garnish. Make the pesto. Tear the remaining leaves into pieces and blend them with the other ingredients for the pesto in a food processor. Transfer to an airtight container until required. **TWO** Cook the noodles according to the instructions on the packet. Rinse under cool running water once, then pour over hot water to reheat. **THREE** Toss the noodles in the pesto and garnish with the reserved shiso and rocket leaves. Serve immediately.

Serves 4

NUTRIENT ANALYSIS PER SERVING 2860 kJ – 614 cal – 17 g protein – 76 g carbohydrate – 6 g sugars – 28 g fat – 3 g saturated fat – 8 g fibre – 1184 mg sodium

HEALTHY TIP Buckwheat, unlike most cereals, is not a grass, but is the seed of a flower. In spite of its name, it is not related to wheat and contains no gluten, so is suitable for those with a gluten allergy or idiosyncrasy.

Tri-colour toppings lunch box *Sanshoku bento* Every morning Japanese mothers make great efforts to provide their children with beautiful lunch boxes to take to school.

INGREDIENTS *600 g (1¼ lb) warm, freshly cooked rice (see page 17)* ‖ *½ sheet of nori, shredded* ‖ *2 teaspoons shoyu*

TOPPING A *250 g (8 oz) skinned fillet of white fish, such as coley, whiting or pollock* ‖ *1 teaspoon mirin* ‖ *1 teaspoon caster sugar* ‖ *1 tablespoon sake or dry sherry* ‖ *1 teaspoon juice from grated fresh root ginger* ‖ *½ teaspoon salt* ‖ *red food colouring*

TOPPING B *3 eggs* ‖ *½ teaspoon salt* ‖ *½ teaspoon vegetable oil*

TOPPING C *100 g (3½ oz) spinach* ‖ *2 teaspoons shoyu*

ONE Make Topping A. Cook the white fish in lightly salted, boiling water. Drain and remove any bones or membranes. Wrap the fish in a tea towel, hold it under cold running water and gently rub the fish through the towel for a few minutes to remove any fat from the fish. Squeeze out the excess liquid. **TWO** Put all the remaining ingredients for Topping A (except the food colouring) in a saucepan. Bring to the boil and add the fish. Reduce the heat to low and use chopsticks or a fork to flake the fish. Stir vigorously until the fish is dry and fluffy. Stir in a drop of red food colouring to make it pink. **THREE** Make Topping B by beating together the eggs and salt. Heat the oil in a small pan and scramble the eggs. Remove from the heat. **FOUR** Make Topping C by cooking the spinach in lightly salted, boiling water for 2 minutes until it turns bright green. Drain and squeeze. Chop roughly and mix with the shoyu. Squeeze again just before use. **FIVE** Half fill 4 lunch boxes or bowls with warm rice. Mix together the nori and shoyu and spread it over the rice. Fill the boxes or bowls with the remaining rice. Press gently to flatten the surface, then arrange the toppings next to each other on top of the rice. This dish can be eaten warm or cold.

Serves 4

NUTRIENT ANALYSIS PER SERVING 1050 kJ – 248 cal – 15 g protein – 46 g carbohydrate – 1 g sugars – 1 g fat – 0 g saturated fat – 1 g fibre – 450 mg sodium

HEALTHY TIP Using all three toppings in one lunch box makes a very nutritious meal. Spinach is particularly high in carotene and folate, and also contains calcium and iron.

Chicken and egg rice bowl *Oyako don* Pieces of stewed chicken are held

in a soft omelette. For a really velvety texture, use very fresh eggs and do not overcook them.

INGREDIENTS *450 ml (¾ pint) Dashi Stock (see page 19)* ‖ *4 tablespoons sake or dry sherry* ‖ *2 tablespoons caster sugar* ‖ *2 tablespoons mirin* ‖ *3 tablespoons shoyu* ‖ *1 onion, thinly sliced* ‖ *350 g (11½ oz) skinless chicken breast, cut into bite-sized pieces* ‖ *6 eggs, beaten* ‖ *20 g (¾ oz) mitsuba leaves or chives, cut into 5 cm (2 inch) pieces* ‖ *600 g (1¼ lb) freshly cooked rice (see page 17)* ‖ *shichimi togarashi (optional)*

ONE In a shallow pan mix together the stock, sake, sugar, mirin and shoyu. Bring to the boil, reduce the heat to medium-low and stir well until the sugar has dissolved. **TWO** Add the onion to the pan and cook for 2 minutes. Add the chicken and simmer for 5–6 minutes or until the meat is cooked. **THREE** Pour the beaten egg over the onion and chicken. After 2 minutes sprinkle the mitsuba over the top. Cook until the egg is almost set but still quite runny. **FOUR** Spoon the rice into 4 donburi (deep bowls) or soup bowls. Carefully scoop the contents of the pan over the rice, sprinkle over some shichimi togarashi, if liked, and serve immediately.

Serves 4

NUTRIENT ANALYSIS PER SERVING 2078 kJ – 493 cal – 34 g protein – 60 g carbohydrate – 13 g sugars – 12 g fat – 3 g saturated fat – 2 g fibre – 860 mg sodium

HEALTHY TIP Eggs are one of the best sources of protein and egg yolks contain iron and vitamins A and D. Egg yolk also contains cholesterol, but provided total fat in the diet is moderate, eggs may be eaten on a regular basis without raising the cholesterol levels in the blood.

Summer-style somen noodles

Soumen Cold and refreshing dishes are essential in the hot and humid Japanese summer. This method of cooking noodles is best for all types of noodle (except ramen noodles) that are used in warm soups. The noodles retain their shape and consistency, and because the excess starch is removed they do not stick together. Try different combinations of condiments in the dipping sauce.

INGREDIENTS *400 g (13 oz) dried somen noodles* ‖ *5–6 shiso leaves or a handful of basil leaves, thinly sliced* ‖ *575 ml (18 fl oz) Tsuyu, recipe B (see page 21)*

TO SERVE *small bunch of chives, finely chopped* ‖ *2.5 cm (1 inch) fresh root ginger, peeled and grated* ‖ *wasabi, to taste*

ONE In a large saucepan bring 2 litres (3½ pints) water to the boil. Drop the noodles into the rapidly boiling water. The water will stop boiling when the noodles are added. When the water begins to bubble again, quickly pour about 100 ml (3½ fl oz) cold water into the pan. Remove from the heat when the surface bubbles up again. It takes only 4–5 minutes. **TWO** Drain the cooked noodles into a sieve and rinse them under cold running water, gently turning the noodles with your hands until they are cold. Drain once, then transfer to a bowl of cold water. Leave to soak. **THREE** Add the shiso leaves to the bowl with the noodles. Take about 20 noodles and wrap around your index finger to make a noodle roll. Arrange the rolls on a plate as you make them. **FOUR** Pour the tsuyu into 4 individual bowls for dipping and serve the noodles with the chives, ginger or wasabi.

Serves 4

NUTRIENT ANALYSIS PER SERVING 1822 kJ – 430 cal – 15 g protein – 80 g carbohydrate – 2 g sugars – 6 g fat – 0 g saturated fat – 6 g fibre – 1480 mg sodium

HEALTHY TIP The high salt content of this recipe is due to the soy sauce. To reduce salt intake look for lower salt varieties.

Redbush tea pilaf with walnuts *Kurumi iri chameshi* This

dish is a variation of rice cooked in tea. Redbush tea has a similar taste to roasted Japanese brown tea but contains no caffeine. The pilaf can be eaten by itself or as an accompaniment to dishes such as Steamed Salmon Parcels with Vegetables *(see page 80)* or Simmered Yams *(see page 107)*.

INGREDIENTS *450 g (14½ oz) white rice, washed and soaked in water for 30 minutes* ‖ *250 ml (8 fl oz) Dashi Stock (see page 19)* ‖ *250 ml (8 fl oz) redbush (rooibos) tea made with 2 teaspoons tea leaves* ‖ *50 ml (2 fl oz) shoyu* ‖ *50 ml (2 fl oz) sake or dry sherry* ‖ *20 g (¾ oz) arame seaweed, washed and drained* ‖ *1 teaspoon walnut or vegetable oil* ‖ *150 g (5 oz) walnut pieces* ‖ *pinch of coarse sea salt*

ONE Drain the rice into a sieve and leave for 30 minutes. Put the rice, stock, tea, shoyu, sake and seaweed into a heavy-based saucepan with a tightly fitting lid. **TWO** Cover the pan and bring the mixture to the boil. Reduce the heat to low and cook until a faint crackling noise comes from the pan. This may take 15–20 minutes. Do not lift the lid. Turn off the heat and keep covered for another 15 minutes. **THREE** Meanwhile, heat the oil in a small, nonstick frying pan and cook the walnut pieces over a low heat until they are crisp. Sprinkle with salt. Fluff up the rice with a rice paddle, mix the walnuts into the rice and serve warm.

Serves 4–6

NUTRIENT ANALYSIS PER SERVING 2930 kJ – 696 cal – 14 g protein – 100 g carbohydrate – 1 g sugars – 28 g fat – 2 g saturated fat – 5 g fibre – 834 mg sodium

HEALTHY TIP Walnuts are high in fat and therefore calories, but they are an excellent source of omega-3 fatty acids which may help to lower blood cholesterol and also have a role in the prevention of clotting.

Crab and vegetable noodles in soup

Kani iri tanmen Get your fishmonger to prepare the crab but ask if you can have the shells for the soup. The best type of crab for this dish is swimming or king crab, but you can use blue, brown, white or spider crabs instead.

INGREDIENTS *3 tablespoons vegetable oil* ‖ *2 spring onions, thinly sliced diagonally* ‖ *cooked meat from 1 crab, 250–325 g (8–11 oz) in total* ‖ *30 g (1¼ oz) shiitake mushrooms, stalks removed and caps thickly sliced* ‖ *50 g (2 oz) cooked bamboo shoots, thinly sliced lengthways* ‖ *50 g (2 oz) mangetout* ‖ *½ red pepper, deseeded and thinly sliced lengthways* ‖ *1 tablespoon sake or dry sherry* ‖ *4 packets fresh or dried thin egg noodles or ramen noodles* ‖ *salt and white pepper*

SOUP *12 prawns, unshelled* ‖ *crab shells* ‖ *3 small dried scallops, soaked in water overnight (optional)* ‖ *1 small onion, quartered* ‖ *5 cm (2 inches) fresh root ginger, unpeeled and crushed* ‖ *3 spring onions, roughly chopped*

ONE Make the soup. In a heavy-based saucepan bring 2.7 litres (5 pints) water to the boil. Add the remaining ingredients and simmer, uncovered, over a medium-low heat for 40 minutes or until the liquid is reduced by half. Skim off the surface scum and strain the soup into a bowl, discarding the solids left in the sieve. Alternatively, shorten the cooking time by using a bottle of good-quality Japanese ramen soup and a seafood or vegetable stock cube to make 1 litre (1¾ pints) soup. **TWO** Heat the oil in a wok or large, nonstick frying pan and fry the spring onions for 2 minutes. Add the crab meat and all the vegetables. Sprinkle over the sake and fry for another 3 minutes. Pour the soup stock into the wok and season with salt to taste. Turn the heat down to the lowest possible setting and keep the soup hot. **THREE** Meanwhile, bring 2 litres (3½ pints) water to the boil and cook the noodles according to the instructions on the packet. Drain the noodles and spoon them into 4 bowls, each deep enough to hold 500 ml (17 fl oz) soup. **FOUR** Pour the soup gently over the noodles, sprinkle with white pepper and serve immediately.

Serves 4

NUTRIENT ANALYSIS PER SERVING 2116 kJ – 503 cal – 24 g protein – 63 g carbohydrate – 2 g sugars – 19 g fat – 1 g saturated fat – 6 g fibre – 884 mg sodium

HEALTHY TIP Crab is comparatively low in fat and is a good source of both copper and zinc, both essential trace minerals. Zinc is necessary for healing wounds and repairing tissue.

Rice and sea bream with Japanese tea

Tai chazuke Hot green tea poured over warm rice, *o-chzuke*, can be a quick snack or a luxurious dish served at the end of a drinking session to mop up the alcohol. The fish has to be fresh enough to be eaten raw.

INGREDIENTS *4 tablespoons toasted white sesame seeds* ‖ *3 tablespoons shoyu* ‖ *250 g (8 oz) fresh red sea bream fillet, cut into 5 mm (¼ inch) slices* ‖ *600 g (1¼ lb) freshly cooked, warm rice (see page 17)* ‖ *4 tablespoons finely chopped chives* ‖ *2 teaspoons wasabi* ‖ *2 tablespoons sencha green tea leaves*

ONE Mix together the sesame seeds and shoyu and marinate the fish slices for 10 minutes. **TWO** Spoon the warm rice into 4 individual bowls. Arrange the fish over the rice and pile chives in the centre with a little wasabi. **THREE** Just before serving, pour 300 ml (½ pint) freshly boiled (but not boiling) water over the tea leaves. Leave to brew for about 2 minutes, then pour the tea carefully over the bowls and serve immediately.

Serves 4

NUTRIENT ANALYSIS PER SERVING 1386 kJ – 329 cal – 18 g protein – 46 g carbohydrate – 0 g sugars – 9 g fat – 1 g saturated fat – 1 g fibre – 719 mg sodium

HEALTHY TIP Green tea is believed to gently increase metabolism (the body's ability to convert food into energy). It also contains anti-oxidants which help to protect against cell damage caused by free radicals.

Cold noodle salad *Hiyashi chuka* It is important to cut all the ingredients in this
salad-style noodle dish to a similar size and shape. This not only looks better but also makes it easier for each
element to blend with the dressing.

INGREDIENTS *1 tablespoon sake or dry sherry* ‖ *400 g (13 oz) chicken breast (with skins)* ‖ *4 packets fresh
or dried thin egg noodles or ramen noodles* ‖ *2 small cucumbers, sliced diagonally and cut into thin strips* ‖
salt ‖ *Japanese or English yellow mustard, to serve*

USUYAKI TAMAGO *1 egg at room temperature* ‖ *vegetable oil, for frying*

DRESSING *8 tablespoons shoyu* ‖ *6 tablespoons caster sugar* ‖ *4 tablespoons rice vinegar* ‖ *2 tablespoons
roasted sesame oil* ‖ *1 tablespoon hot chilli sesame oil*

TO GARNISH *2 tomatoes, cut into 8 segments* ‖ *3 tablespoons Beni Shoga (see page 21)*

ONE Lightly beat the egg. Heat about ½ tablespoon oil in a small pan. When it is hot, remove it from the
heat and cool it down slightly. Wipe away excess oil with kitchen paper. Carefully pour the egg into the pan
so that it thinly covers the surface, tilting the pan for even coverage. Return the pan to a medium-low heat
and when the surface starts to look dry, turn or flip the omelette over. Cook for a further 30 seconds. Leave
to cool and cut into thin strips. **TWO** Bring 250 ml (8 fl oz) water to the boil. Add the sake, a pinch of salt
and the chicken, then simmer for 10 minutes over medium-low heat. Leave to cool. Drain and remove the
skin from the chicken and tear the flesh into strips. **THREE** Make the dressing by mixing together all the
ingredients. Keep in the refrigerator until required. **FOUR** Cook the noodles in boiling water according to
the instructions on the packet. Wash under running water until they are cold. Drain and transfer to 4 plates.
FIVE Arrange strips of cucumber, chicken and omelette over the noodles and garnish with tomatoes and
beni shoga. Pour the dressing over the noodles and serve immediately. Mix some mustard to taste.

Serves 4

NUTRIENT ANALYSIS PER SERVING 3392 kJ – 807 cal – 33 g protein – 94 g carbohydrate – 34 g sugars –
36 g fat – 8 g saturated fat – 5 g fibre – 2154 mg sodium

HEALTHY TIP Reduce the sugar content of this dish by substituting light sugar for ordinary cane sugar.

Noodles with chicken, prawns and baby leeks

Chasoba nanban Noodles flavoured with green tea are the main ingredient in this dish. The tea's fragrance complements the subtle flavours of the tsuyu and prawns.

INGREDIENTS *1 teaspoon vegetable oil* ‖ *2 boneless, skinless chicken thighs, cut into bite-sized pieces* ‖ *3 baby leeks, cut into 5 cm (2 inch) pieces* ‖ *2 litres (3½ pints) Tsuyu, recipe A (see page 20)* ‖ *400 g (13 oz) dried cha-soba (green tea flavoured) noodles or plain soba (buckwheat) noodles* ‖ *100 g (3½ oz) large cooked peeled prawns, cut into 1 cm (½ inch) pieces* ‖ *shichimi togarashi, to serve (optional)*

ONE Heat the oil in a large, nonstick frying pan and fry the chicken and leeks over a high heat for 5 minutes. Reduce the heat to moderate and add the tsuyu. Sautée until the chicken is completely cooked. Remove from the heat and set aside. **TWO** Cook the noodles in boiling water according to the instructions on the packet. Drain under cold running water, turning the noodles with your hands until they are cold. **THREE** Heat the tsuyu until it is hot but not boiling, then add the noodles and prawns to reheat. Sprinkle with shichimi togarashi, if liked, and serve immediately.

Serves 4

NUTRIENT ANALYSIS PER SERVING 2154 kJ – 440 cal – 25 g protein – 76 g carbohydrate – 6 g sugars – 4 g fat – 1 g saturated fat – 6 g fibre – 2040 mg sodium

HEALTHY TIP Leeks are a good source of dietary fibre and contain useful amounts of carotene, which has important anti-oxidant properties.

Desserts

Sweet chestnut dumplings *Kuri manjyu*

Nuts, sweet potatoes, kabocha pumpkins and pulses are common ingredients in sweet dishes in Japan. Often sweetened only with sugar or rice syrup, the uncomplicated taste compliments the slightly bitter taste of green tea.

INGREDIENTS *375 g (12 oz) fresh chestnuts, unpeeled* ‖ *200 g (7 oz) sweet potato, peeled* ‖ *4 tablespoons milk* ‖ *25 g (1 oz) butter or margarine* ‖ *1 tablespoon unrefined icing sugar* ‖ *50 g (2 oz) somen noodles, cut into 2 cm (¾ inch) lengths* ‖ *vegetable oil, for frying*

ONE Steam the whole chestnuts and sweet potato for 15 minutes or until they are cooked thorough. When they have cooled slightly, reserve 12 chestnuts and peel off the skins. Cut each of the remaining chestnuts in half and scoop out the cooked flesh. Mash it through a sieve. **TWO** Mash the sweet potato with the milk, butter and sugar. Put the mixture in a saucepan and stir over low heat. Add the mashed chestnut and mix well for 2–3 minutes until the mixture thickens a little. **THREE** Place a wet tea towel over your palm and put 4–5 tablespoons chestnut mixture on it. Gently wrap and squeeze the cloth to make a ball about 5 cm (2 inches) across. Open the cloth, push a chestnut inside it and rewrap to make a ball. Repeat to make 12 more dumplings. Set aside. **FOUR** Heat oil to a depth of 2.5 cm (1 inch) in a pan to 180°C (350°F). Fry the noodles for 1 minute or until they are golden. Drain on kitchen paper. **FIVE** Coat the dumplings with fried somen. Score them from top to bottom and arrange them on a plate so that they resemble opened chestnut shells.

Makes 12 dumplings; serves 4–6

NUTRIENT ANALYSIS PER SERVING 1309 kJ – 310 cal – 4 g protein – 54 g carbohydrate – 15 g sugars – 10 g fat – 4 g saturated fat – 7 g fibre – 106 mg sodium

HEALTHY TIP Chestnuts are a good source of starch and sugar and contain small amounts of vitamins and minerals. Orange-fleshed sweet potato is very high in the anti-oxidant carotene, white-fleshed sweet potatoes have lower levels of carotene.

Fig cake *Ichijiku yaki gashi*

Figs are often used in oriental medicinal cooking, especially in sweet dishes. This recipe, which is suitable for vegans, contains amaranthus seeds, which enhance the crunchy texture of the fig seeds. If you prefer, use 8 dried figs and soak them in the soya milk overnight, adding an extra 50 ml (2 fl oz) milk to the recipe.

INGREDIENTS *180 g (6¼ oz) plain wholemeal flour* ‖ *½ teaspoon baking powder* ‖ *4 tablespoons vegetable oil* ‖ *75 ml (3 fl oz) umeshu (plum wine)* ‖ *75 ml (3 fl oz) maple syrup* ‖ *1½ teaspoons cider vinegar* ‖ *125 ml (4 fl oz) sweetened soya milk* ‖ *1 tablespoon amaranthus seeds* ‖ *4 fresh figs, about 200 g (7 oz) in total, cut into 5 mm (¼ inch) slices* ‖ *salt* ‖ *crème fraîche (optional)*

ONE Sift the flour, baking powder and a pinch of salt into a bowl. Tip the bran left in the sieve into the bowl. **TWO** Add all the other ingredients (except the figs) to the bowl and stir to combine but do not whisk. Lightly oil a cake tin, 20 cm (8 inches) across and 4 cm (1½ inches) deep. Pour in the mixture. **THREE** Place the figs on top of the cake and bake in a preheated oven, 180°C (350°F), Gas Mark 4, for 35–40 minutes. Leave to cool and serve with a drop of crème fraîche, if preferred. This cake can be served with a Japanese tea, such as hoji.

Serves 4

NUTRIENT ANALYSIS PER SERVING 1405 kJ – 335 cal – 8 g protein – 48 g carbohydrate – 18 g sugars – 13 g fat – 1 g saturated fat – 5 g fibre – 84 mg sodium

HEALTHY TIP Figs are a good hangover cure. They contain an enzyme that helps to break down the alcohol and stimulate the body's metabolism. They are also known to contain benxaldehyde, which may help to prevent some cancers.

Aduki bean and nut pie

Anko to kinomi pai This pie is a modern version of a traditional cake, in which the sweet aduki paste is encased in a thin crust made of rice flour. The low-fat pie crust can be used for any of the pie recipes.

INGREDIENTS *200 g (7 oz) cooked aduki beans (see page 12)* ‖ *80 g (3¼ oz) caster sugar* ‖ *150 g (5 oz) roasted mixed nuts, coarsely chopped* ‖ *salt*

PIE CRUST *50 g (2 oz) rolled oats* ‖ *20 g (¾ oz) puffed rice* ‖ *3 tablespoons honey* ‖ *1 teaspoon vegetable oil* ‖ *½ teaspoon salt* ‖ *80 g (3¼ oz) plain flour*

ONE Put the beans in a heavy-based saucepan with 200 ml (7 fl oz) water over a low heat. Add the sugar in 3 batches, stirring constantly until it has dissolved. Increase the heat to medium. Add a pinch of salt and stir until the mixture becomes a moist mash. Remove from the heat. **TWO** Make the pie crust. Put the oats and puffed rice in a plastic bag and crush them with a rolling pin. Mix together the honey, oil and salt in a bowl with 2½ tablespoons water, then add the flour, oats and puffed rice to make a crumble. Blend well and leave for 10 minutes. **THREE** Use your fingertips to press the crumble into a lightly oiled, fluted flan tin 20 cm (8 inches) across. (If there is extra crumble, flatten it and place it on an oiled baking sheet.) Bake in a preheated oven, 230°C (450°F), Gas Mark 8, for 15 minutes or until it is dry and golden. Leave to cool before removing the case from the tin. **FOUR** Fill the pie case with the aduki mash and coat the surface with nuts. Any extra pie crust from step 3 can be crumbled and sprinkled over the top. Serve with hot or cold green tea.

Serves 6–8

NUTRIENT ANALYSIS PER SERVING 1544 kJ – 366 cal – 11 g protein – 56 g carbohydrate – 25 g sugars – 13 g fat – 1 g saturated fat – 2 g fibre – 210 mg sodium

HEALTHY TIP Oats are an important source of soluble fibre which helps prevent bowel cancer and other intestinal problems.

Creamy tofu cheesecake

Tofu is an amazingly versatile, nutritious and healthy ingredient. It can be substituted for dairy foods in savoury or sweet dishes, as it is in this one. The problem with this fluffy cheesecake is that it is completely irresistible.

INGREDIENTS *250 ml (8 fl oz) plain yogurt* ‖ *200 g (7 oz) firm tofu* ‖ *25 g (1 oz) unsalted butter or margarine, at room temperature* ‖ *3 eggs, separated* ‖ *1 tablespoon lemon juice* ‖ *2 teaspoons rum* ‖ *30 g (1¼ oz) plain flour, sifted* ‖ *2 tablespoons caster sugar* ‖ *2 tablespoons apricot jam*

ONE Place a sieve over a bowl, line it with muslin and pour in the yogurt. Leave it overnight to drain out the moisture (whey). **TWO** Put the tofu between two tea towels and place a chopping board on top. Leave for 1 hour to remove the excess water. **THREE** Blend the tofu, yogurt and butter in a food processor. Transfer to a large bowl and mix in the egg yolks, then add the lemon juice, rum and flour. **FOUR** In a separate bowl whisk the egg whites until they form stiff peaks, then add the sugar in 3 batches. Gently fold the egg whites into the tofu mixture and pour the mixture into a lightly oiled, round cake tin. **FIVE** Pour hot water to a depth of 2.5 cm (1 inch) into a baking tin. Stand the cake tin on a metal grid or trivet and bake the cheesecake in a preheated oven, 160°C (325°F), Gas Mark 3, for 50 minutes or until a skewer inserted in the middle comes out dry. Leave to cool. **SIX** Mix the apricot jam with ½ tablespoon water and brush the top of the cheesecake with the mixture before serving.

Serves 4–6

NUTRIENT ANALYSIS PER SERVING 1180 kJ – 282 cal – 13 g protein – 30 g carbohydrate – 24 g sugars – 12 g fat – 5 g saturated fat – 1 g fibre – 120 mg sodium

HEALTHY TIP As cheesecakes go this one is relatively low in fat and is loaded with calcium, essential for bone growth and repair. Egg yolks are a good source of dietary vitamin D, which is also essential for strong, healthy bones.

Green tea chiffon cake *Maccha keki* Maccha, powdered green tea, is mainly served at tea ceremonies and is not an everyday drink in Japanese homes. However, it is widely used as a flavouring in cakes, ice creams and even green milkshakes. Fruit sugar, which is available in health-food stores and large supermarkets, is 30 per cent sweeter than cane sugar and therefore less is needed.

INGREDIENTS *3 eggs, separated, and 1 egg white* ‖ *3 tablespoons fruit sugar* ‖ *2 tablespoons vegetable oil* ‖ *80 g (3¼ oz) plain flour, sifted* ‖ *1 tablespoon maccha (powdered green tea)* ‖ *crème fraîche, to serve (optional)*

ONE Put the egg yolks and 1 tablespoon sugar in a bowl and whisk to make a smooth cream. Gradually mix in the oil, then 2 tablespoons water. Add the flour and maccha and mix well. **TWO** Put the egg whites in a large bowl and whisk until the mixture forms peaks when the whisk is lifted. Add the remaining sugar in 2 batches and continue to whisk until the mixture becomes a meringue. **THREE** Fold the meringue into the egg yolk mixture in 3 batches, using a cutting motion with a spatula to keep the mixture foamy. **FOUR** Pour the mixture into a lightly oiled ring tin, 18 cm (7 inches) across, and bake in a preheated oven, 180°C (350°F), Gas Mark 4, for 15 minutes. Reduce the temperature to 160°C (325°F), Gas Mark 3, and cook for a further 20–25 minutes. Insert a skewer and if it comes out dry, the cake is cooked. Remove from the oven and leave to cool. **FIVE** Remove the cake from the tin and leave to cool. Serve it by itself or with a spoonful of crème fraîche.

Serves 4–6

NUTRIENT ANALYSIS PER SERVING 1016 kJ – 242 cal – 8 g protein – 32 g carbohydrate – 16 g sugars – 10 g fat – 2 g saturated fat – 1 g fibre – 74 mg sodium

HEALTHY TIP Maccha is rich in vitamin C and minerals.

Japanese-style pancake rolls

Amai fukusa Adding sake to the batter makes this pancake moist and gives an interesting flavour.

INGREDIENTS *200 g (7 oz) cooked aduki beans (see page 12)* ‖ *80 g (3¼ oz) caster sugar* ‖ *50 g (2 oz) walnuts, roughly crushed* ‖ *150 g (5 oz) plain flour* ‖ *5 tablespoons caster sugar* ‖ *½ teaspoon baking soda* ‖ *1 egg, beaten* ‖ *1 tablespoon sake* ‖ *1 tablespoon crème fraîche* ‖ *2 teaspoons vegetable oil* ‖ *salt*

VANILLA SAUCE *6 tablespoons good quality vanilla ice cream, melted* ‖ *pinch of ground star anise*

ONE Put the beans in a heavy-based saucepan with 200 ml (7 fl oz) water over a low heat. Add the sugar in 3 batches, stirring constantly until it has dissolved. Increase the heat to medium-low. Add a pinch of salt and stir until the mixture becomes a moist mash. **TWO** Dry-fry the walnuts in a nonstick frying pan for 5 minutes until they are golden. Leave to cool then mix with the bean mash. **THREE** Sift the flour, sugar and baking soda into a large bowl. Add 125 ml (4 fl oz) water and the egg, sake and crème fraîche and mix together lightly. **FOUR** Heat half the oil a frying pan until it starts to smoke. Remove from heat and set the pan on a wet tea towel to cool for 15 seconds. Bring back to a low heat and pour in half the crème fraîche mixture to make a pancake about 20 cm (8 inches) across. Cook the pancake until the underside is brown, then turn to cook the other side for 1 minute so that it is paler. Repeat to make 2 pancakes. **FIVE** Place a pancake on a makisu mat, brown side up. Spread over half the aduki mash and roll up the pancake as if making a Swiss roll. Hold the rolled mat in place with 2 elastic bands and let it settle for 5 minutes. Repeat to make another roll. **SIX** Mix the ice cream and star anise powder to make a vanilla sauce. Slice each roll into 6 pieces and serve with the sauce.

Serves 4

NUTRIENT ANALYSIS PER SERVING 2519 kJ – 597 cal – 14 g protein – 99 g carbohydrate – 69 g sugars – 19 g fat – 6 g saturated fat – 4 g fibre – 190 mg sodium

HEALTHY TIP To reduce the sugar content of this recipe, light sugar could be used instead of ordinary cane sugar.

Black sesame ice cream with beetroot chips *Kuro goma aisu*

Only a few years ago, the grey colour of this ice cream shocked diners when a top restaurant in Tokyo, known for its innovative dishes, started to offer it. The earthy taste of black sesame and ice cream is a divine combination, and imitations quickly appeared everywhere in Japan. Now it is being made around the world.

INGREDIENTS *2 egg yolks* ‖ *4 tablespoons caster sugar* ‖ *150 ml (¼ pint) soya milk or milk* ‖ *200 ml (7 fl oz) double cream* ‖ *4 tablespoons black sesame tahini (Kuro neri goma) or 6 tablespoons black sesame seeds ground with a Suribachi* ‖ *1 beetroot, peeled and thinly sliced* ‖ *vegetable oil, for greasing*

ONE Whisk together the egg yolks and sugar until smooth. Add the milk. **TWO** Whisk the cream until it forms soft peaks, then fold it into the egg and milk mixture. Add the tahini and blend well, then transfer the mixture to the freezer for 3 hours, stirring every 30 minutes. **THREE** Dry the beetroot slices between pieces of kitchen paper for 15 minutes. Line a baking sheet with lightly oiled greaseproof paper and spread the slices evenly over the surface. Bake in a preheated oven, 200°C (400°F), Gas Mark 6, for 15–20 minutes or until they are crisp. **FOUR** Decorate the ice cream with beetroot chips and serve immediately.

Serves 4

NUTRIENT ANALYSIS PER SERVING 2050 kJ – 494 cal – 8 g protein – 24 g carbohydrate – 24 g sugars – 42 g fat – 18 g saturated fat – 0 g fibre – 48 mg sodium

HEALTHY TIP Milk and tahini are both good sources of calcium, necessary for bone growth and maintenance. If using soya milk, check that it has a high calcium content.

Baked sweet potato with apple sauce *Daigaku imo* This

dish is a teatime favourite among older ladies in Japan. A little shoyu gives the sweet potatoes a slightly

spicy aroma.

INGREDIENTS *2 sweet potatoes, washed and soaked in cold water for 20 minutes* ‖ *1 tablespoon vegetable oil* ‖ *1½ tablespoons demerara sugar* ‖ *½ teaspoon shoyu* ‖ *1 teaspoon black sesame seeds*

APPLE SAUCE *1 large cooking apple, peeled, cored and roughly chopped* ‖ *2 tablespoons honey* ‖ *1 tablespoon lemon juice*

ONE Make the apple sauce. Mix together the ingredients with 100 ml (3½ fl oz) water and cook over low heat for 15–20 minutes until the apple becomes pulpy. Set aside to cool. **TWO** Drain and wipe the sweet potatoes. Cut them into bite-sized pieces and place them in a large bowl. Drizzle over the oil and toss to coat the surface of the potatoes. **THREE** Bake the potatoes in a preheated oven, 230°C (450°F), Gas Mark 8, on a high shelf for 25–35 minutes until they are browned and a skewer can easily be inserted. **FOUR** Put the sugar and shoyu in a frying pan, add 1½ tablespoons water and bring to the boil. Stir until the sugar has dissolved and the mixture is starting to bubble. Add the cooked potatoes and shake the pan vigorously to coat them with the liquid. **FIVE** Remove from the heat and spread the potatoes on a large tray to cool. Serve on a bed of apple sauce and sprinkled with sesame seeds.

Serves 4

NUTRIENT ANALYSIS PER SERVING 1808 kJ – 254 cal – 3 g protein – 56 g carbohydrate – 24 g sugars – 4 g fat – 1 g saturated fat – 5 g fibre – 125 mg sodium

HEALTHY TIP Orange-fleshed sweet potatoes have a very high carotene content and are also a good source of vitamin E, which has anti-oxidant properties.

Persimmon compote with yogurt mousse *Kaki to*

yoguruto musu Fruit compote is a good way to use up ripe fruits when you have too many to eat fresh. Peaches, pears or plums can be used instead of persimmons in this dish. Some types of persimmon break down into a pulp when they are cooked, but they taste just as good as the firm types. Use the pulp as a sauce for the mousse.

INGREDIENTS *4 tablespoons white wine* ‖ *1 tablespoon caster sugar* ‖ *1 tablespoon lemon juice* ‖ *450 g (14½ oz) ripe kaki (persimmons), peeled, cored and thinly sliced lengthways*

YOGURT MOUSSE *50 ml (2 fl oz) milk* ‖ *2 tablespoons caster sugar* ‖ *5 g (¼ oz) gelatine* ‖ *100 ml (3½ fl oz) single cream* ‖ *200 ml (7 fl oz) plain yogurt* ‖ *grated rind of ¼ lemon*

ONE Mix together the wine, sugar and lemon juice in a saucepan. Add 200 ml (7 fl oz) water and bring to the boil. Add the persimmons and cook for 5 minutes over a low heat. Leave to cool. **TWO** Make the mousse. Heat the milk in a saucepan and add the sugar. Mix the gelatine in 2 tablespoons water and stir until it has dissolved. Add to the milk, stir to combine and remove from the heat. Leave to cool. **THREE** Whip the cream until it forms peaks when the whisk is lifted. Stir in the yogurt and lemon rind, add the gelatine mixture and mix well. Pour into a plastic container and leave to set in the refrigerator for 1 hour. Whisk again and return to the refrigerator for a further hour. Serve the mousse with the compote.

Serves 4

NUTRIENT ANALYSIS PER SERVING 1000 kJ – 239 cal – 6 g protein – 42 g carbohydrate – 42 g sugars – 5 g fat –3 g saturated fat – 0 g fibre – 70 mg sodium

HEALTHY TIP Like tomatoes, persimmons (also called kaki fruit/Sharon fruit) contain lycopene, a carotenoid compound that acts as an anti-oxidant. Lycopene may help protect against bladder and pancreatic cancers.

Plum wine jelly with ginger and lemon sorbet

Umeshu kanten In Japan this jelly is traditionally served as an afternoon snack with tea, but it can also be offered as a refreshing dessert. The gelatinous agar-agar is derived from various kinds of red seaweed and is thus suitable for vegetarians.

INGREDIENTS *handful of almond macaroons, finely crushed* ‖ *6 tablespoons crème fraîche* ‖ *4 sprigs of lemon balm or mint, to decorate*

JELLY *1 teaspoon agar-agar (powder or flakes)* ‖ *75 g (3 oz) caster sugar* ‖ *75 ml (3 fl oz) umeshu (plum wine)*

SORBET *3 tablespoons granulated sugar* ‖ *3 tablespoons lemon juice* ‖ *grated rind of ½ lemon* ‖ *juice from 2.5 cm (1 inch) fresh root ginger, peeled, crushed and squeezed*

ONE Make the jelly. Put the agar-agar with 200 ml (7 fl oz) water in a small saucepan and bring to the boil, stirring constantly with a whisk. Reduce the heat to medium and cook for 2 minutes, stirring. Remove from heat, add the sugar and stir. Leave to cool for 15 minutes, then stir in the wine. Pour into a plastic container and leave at room temperature for 1½ hours until it sets. Mash the jelly with a fork. **TWO** Make the sorbet. Put the sugar in a small saucepan, add 3 tablespoons water and heat gently until the sugar has dissolved. Leave to cool, stir in the lemon juice with the rind and ginger juice. Transfer to a plastic container and freeze, beating in a food processor or whisking by hand once an hour for 3 hours. **THREE** Mix the crushed almond macaroons with the crème fraîche. Spoon 2 tablespoons jelly into 4 champagne flutes, add a quarter of the crème fraîche, then another 2 tablespoons of jelly. Top with the sorbet and decorate with a sprig of lemon balm. Serve immediately.

Serves 4

NUTRIENT ANALYSIS PER SERVING 1178 kJ – 280 cal – 1 g protein – 40 g carbohydrate – 39 g sugars – 13 g fat – 8 g saturated fat – 0 g fibre – 4 mg sodium

HEALTHY TIP To reduce the fat content of this dessert, use half-fat crème fraîche.

Index

Acknowledgements

AUTHOR ACKNOWLEDGEMENTS My heartfelt thanks to Sophia Dunn, Meg Komiya and Chinami Taniguchi for their help and friendship. Thanks to Björn Hagert for his encouragement. Lastly, thanks to my parents in Tokyo and all the restaurants and Izakaya (bars) in Japan that I ever visited for the inspiration for these recipes

Japanese knives supplied for photography courtesy of Nippon Kitchen, nipponkitchen.com

EXECUTIVE EDITOR Nicky Hill
EDITOR Charlotte Macey
DEPUTY CREATIVE DIRECTOR AND DESIGN Geoff Fennell
PHOTOGRAPHY Stephen Conroy
FOOD STYLIST Yasuko Fukuoka
FOOD STYLING ASSISTANCE Mari Kobayashi
PROP STYLIST Liz Hippisley
SENIOR PRODUCTION CONTROLLER Manjit Sihra